LETTERS ON PROBABILITY

LETTERS ON PROBABILITY

by

ALFRÉD RÉNYI

translated by

LÁSZLÓ VEKERDI

WAYNE STATE UNIVERSITY PRESS DETROIT 1972

Title of the Hungarian edition: *Levelek a valószínűségről*
Title of the German edition: *Briefe über die Wahrscheinlichkeit*

Copyright © Akadémiai Kiadó, Budapest, 1969

Translation into English published jointly by Wayne State University Press,
Detroit, Michigan 48202 and Akadémiai Kiadó, Budapest

Copyright © 1972 by Akadémiai Kiadó, Budapest, Hungary

All rights reserved.
Library of Congress Catalog Card Number 74—179559

nternational Standard Book Number 0—8143—1465—1

ibrary of Congress Cataloging in Publication Data

Rényi, Alfréd.
  Letters on probability.

  Translation of Levelek a valószínűségről.
  Includes bibliographical references.
  1. Probabilities. 2. Fermat, Pierre de, 1601—1665.
3. Pascal, Blaise, 1623—1662. I. Title.

QA274.13.L4813 519.2 74—179559
ISBN 0—8143—1465—1

Printed in Hungary at Akadémiai Nyomda

CONTENTS

PREFACE

Let the following correspondence serve as preface.

Prof. Dr. Alfréd Rényi
Budapest

Dear Professor Rényi,

Do you remember our talk during the Pascal Memorial Symposium in Clermont-Ferrand, on June 9, 1962? I am not sure I recall it exactly; allow me therefore to return to some particulars of our conversation. On that day we participants of the congress made a trip to the peak of the Puy de Dôme, where Monsieur Périer performed the famous experiment on air pressure planned by his brother-in-law, Blaise Pascal. As we were sitting about on the terrace of the restaurant, drinking our coffee and enjoying the wonderful panorama, the discussion of course turned to Pascal, especially to the question of which one of his works might have most decisively influenced the development of science. Perhaps his investigations in aerodynamics and hydrodynamics? Or the construction of the first calculating machine? Or his research on the foundation of calculus? But was he not still more influential in the creation of the calculus of probabilities?

Meanwhile I hinted at a letter of Pascal dated 1654, which he directed towards the so-called Parisian Academy, founded by Marin Mersenne (and after his death in 1648 administered by M. La Pailleur), in which he enumerated some of his nearly completed works shortly to be presented to the Academy. Among these, Pascal mentions a treatise on an entirely new theme, the Mathematics of Chance, never systematically dealt with by anybody thus far. I expressed the opinion that Pascal's few lines sketching the plan of the treatise suggest his complete awareness of the practical as well as of the fundamental importance of this new doctrine, the calculus of probabilities. Furthermore, I said it was a pity that Pascal never wrote this planned treatise, the more so, because his few hints at probability calculus — namely, his letters to Fermat — are much too short and are limited to the solution of the problems of Chevalier de Méré (and to the combinatorial problems connected with them). Without the above-mentioned letter to the Academy of Paris, we could even ignore if Pascal was aware

3

that he and Fermat had created the basis of a new science which in its later development was destined to transform our whole scientific attitude.

Let me remind you that you considered it quite impossible that Pascal would not have written down his thoughts on probability and that your proposed search be made for the missing manuscript. I answered that Pascal's surviving writings have already been very carefully explored, in fact more carefully than those of very few other men. I have spent some years in the archives searching after other manuscripts of Pascal, unfortunately without any reasonable success. You persisted in your opinion, however, and suggested that Pascal might have perfected this missing treatise – as was common in those times – in the form of letters; perhaps his known letters to Fermat on dicing may not be the only ones about this theme: the correspondence might have been continued. You added that the futility of the search could be explained in that the missing treatise had always been looked for among the surviving manuscripts of Pascal instead of further letters of Pascal being sought for among the surviving papers of Fermat.

In those days I mused over your remark, and it seemed to me plausible enough. But, busy with a lot of other things, I could not dwell upon your idea, and I thought little more about it until 1966, when I had to go to Toulouse because of a family affair. An uncle of mine – a rather funny old bachelor – died and made me heir to his estate in Toulouse under the condition that I must publish the proceedings of a lawsuit conducted 300 years ago concerning this same estate. I wished to fulfill the last demand of my uncle conscientiously, not just as a duty but because I have always been intensely interested in the history of my family. Thus in January of this year I went to Toulouse and rummaged in the Municipal Archives through the law-court papers for the years around 1660. As you know I have spent some years studying Pascal's manuscripts, so that I literally know his handwriting better than my own. Thus you must not be surprised that as soon as I came across a manuscript of Pascal – on the evening of January 17, while turning over the files of documents, signed among others by Fermat – I identified it by his handwriting immediately. You can imagine my enthusiastic joy! I did not leave the Archives until the following morning. Without eating or drinking, I continued the search, and I have found three further letters. Later on I realized that after Fermat's death all these letters had been put among the official documents found in his home and — on January 17, 1665 — were brought to the Archives where they have been lying for 301 years without being disturbed by anyone.

Thus by chance I became the happy possessor of these letters, which are of paramount importance both scientifically and historically. Of course, the discovery is really not so much to my credit; I was simply lucky. It was you who was the first to suggest that Pascal might have written his treatise on probability in the form of letters to Fermat, so that I looked for these letters in the papers left by Fermat. In my opinion, therefore, it is your privilege to publish them.

I hereby send you the copies of the letters. I have carefully read and corrected them all. However, I must leave the great work of editing entirely to you alone and without my help.

Perhaps you are somewhat surprised by my decision, but if I tell you the reason for it, you will understand promptly. Among the papers I have found some pages with number-theoretic content in the handwriting of Fermat. Those pages are almost completely written in symbols, almost without text; yet even so, it is clear that they are associated with Fermat's great theorem. Now I am working day and night on the decoding of these records. I hope that either I can find Fermat's missing proof of the theorem, or that I can prove that he did not prove his theorem, i.e., that his supposed proof was false and that in his last years he himself was aware of this fact. You will understand that I am so interested in this problem that I cannot turn to anything else before it is solved. Originally, just after finding Pascal's letters, my intention was to publish them together with a detailed essay. But before I could begin the essay, Fermat's notes came into my hands and since then I have been occupied only by them. Only after solving the puzzle on these pages, shall I perhaps have the leisure to write my planned essay on Pascal's letters. The publishing of the letters of Pascal should not be delayed, however, and, thus, I ask you to arrange for the publication of them as soon as possible.

I thank you, dear friend, in advance and remain,

Yours sincerely,

Henri Trouverien

Professor of the History of Mathematics
University of Contebleu

Budapest, April 10, 1966

Professor Dr. Henri Trouverien
Chimères

Dear Professor Trouverien,
I have gratefully received your kind letter of April 1 with the letters of Pascal. Of course, I shall with the greatest of pleasure comply with your wish. I ask your permission to publish your letter to me with Pascal's letters, so that the scientific world will know that you were the discoverer of these letters and will see how everything came about. It is far from my intention to divert you from your great work on the deciphering of Fermat's notes. I and all of my fellow mathematicians in Hungary wish you much success in this work and await its results with the greatest interest. Still I should like to ask you one question: namely, do you believe that there is some hope of also finding Fermat's answers to the letters of Pascal?

Yours sincerely,

Alfréd Rényi

Chimères, May 3, 1966

Professor Dr. Alfréd Rényi
Budapest

Dear Professor Rényi,

Thank you very much for your letter of April 10. I am indeed happy that I succeeded in persuading you to work on the edition of Pascal's letters. Thus you have taken this task from my shoulders and I can concentrate with all my strength on the decoding of Fermat's notes. Unfortunately, this is a harder task than I suspected at the beginning; Fermat used quite uncommon symbols and I am still at the very beginning of the deciphering. Naturally, I have nothing against the publication of my previous letter (as well as of this) with the letters of Pascal. As for the answers of Fermat, however, I have no hope of finding them. After Pascal's death all of his papers fell into the hands of his sister Gilberte Périer and she – while carefully preserving (and even copying) everything written by Pascal – unfortunately destroyed all letters sent to him. Thus, the contents of Fermat's letters can only be guessed at from the answers of Pascal.

Sincerely your friend,

Henri Trouverien

PASCAL'S LETTERS TO FERMAT

Paris, Faubourg Saint-Michel,
                             October 28, 1654

                             M. Pierre Fermat
                             Toulouse

Sir,

   Our common friend M. de Carcavi informed me yesterday evening
about his departure for Toulouse and asked me if I wished to send
you a letter. Naturally, I could not resist such a convenient opportunity although I did not find the time to write more than a few
lines.[1] But today it appeared that M. de Carcavi had to delay his
journey for two days and thus I was given the chance to write at
greater length.

   It is now more than a year since the problems posed by the Chevalier
de Méré — on a trip to Poitou, in the company of the Duke de Roanne
and M. Miton — are completely clarified and I must confess that our
friendship, which became established through the correspondence
about these problems, caused me much more joy than the solution
of the problems. In fact, I value your friendship, Sir, above everything,
and not only because you are the best geometrician[2] in the whole of
Europe but through your letters I have also become acquainted with
a man whose friendship even kings could be proud of. Thus, the
questions of the good Chevalier — even if they were not of much interest in themselves — rendered an invaluable service to me. But just
because your friendship is so important to me, I should like to share
all of my thoughts with you. I cannot refrain from telling you why I
am so intensely interested in these questions and why — what is more,
for two different reasons — I consider them worthy of the attention of
every mathematician; so much so that I dared to demand from you
the solution of these problems, although I thereby took upon myself
the responsibility of diverting you from your other investigations,
which no one esteems more highly than I do. As I have said, in this
respect my conscience is entirely clear; still I believe that I owe you
an explanation, primarily because in our past correspondence the
significance of such problems did not appear at all. Considerations
of this kind have induced me to write this letter to you.

   I have a further reason for it, however. I suppose you know my
letter which I wrote for the Academy of Paris some weeks ago;[3]

it would not surprise me if the following sentence, in which I wished to outline the contents of a planned but not yet finished treatise, would seem somewhat like boasting to you: "This doctrine, joining the exactness of the mathematical demonstration to the uncertainty of chance and thus bringing together these two apparently very contradictory elements, can then rightly be designated through a borrowing of the names of both contrary constituents: the mathematics of chance."[4] I wrote these lines immediately after I mentally organized the ideas which I try to summarize below.

I am reminded by my own words, as I now read them again, of the feeling of triumph which filled me when I finished the writing of these lines: the rejoicing over the discovery that a new branch of mathematics — and, as I dare to hope, one with a good future — is coming into being here. I would not be surprised if you were to blame me because my joy was conditioned by the pride I felt that I myself was fortunate enough to assist at the birth of this new mathematical discipline. Though this kind of pride is among the human weaknesses of which I am certainly not free — although I constantly try to suppress them in myself — I must hasten to state that I deem your role in the creation of this new branch of mathematics certainly to be far more important than my own. Thus I am sure that in everything which I write in my present letter, imperfectly formulated as it may be, you will recognize your own ideas which — though perhaps up to now not yet written down or even explicitly formulated — were developed and crystallized in your mind long ago. Undoubtedly my formulations are not completely mature, but in my defense I can say that even the words to express my ideas failed me, so that I saw myself forced to create these expressions myself, i.e., I had to take them over from the vernacular and endow them with a new and precise meaning.

I believe you understand completely why I am driven by a nearly irresistible desire to communicate my ideas to you. But I admit that you may find it less understandable why I make these lengthy apologies. Nevertheless, you will understand if you try to imagine my state of mind, which I should indeed like to ask you to do. You are the first to whom I am disclosing my ideas, and, although there is nobody else from whom I could hope for more understanding, I am still not free of a certain fear that I cannot always express myself quite intelligibly. Therefore, I hesitate to begin, like somebody at the dentist's who, just before the extraction of his aching tooth, gabbles about all his pains in order to gain some time. But enough of this: to the subject!

To my mind, man is born to think. His ability to think distinguishes him from animals; on this rests his human dignity.[5] We are surrounded by a twofold infinity: On the one hand, there lurk around us the infinite distances of the Universe, in which not only we and our Earth but also the Sun and the Planets are, as it were, only minute drops in the ocean; and, on the other hand, there are the infinite depths of the world where each small drop of water forms a little Universe in itself. We find ourselves in the middle between the infinitely large and the infinitely small; we are as grains of dust with respect to the stars but as giants with respect to the small living things which swarm in a drop of water.[6] It is immaterial whether we raise our eyes to the stars or cast them down into our own soul, whether we want to search into the future or into the past: nowhere can we find a strong foothold. In considering something more closely which we believe we know — fixing it with the point of our attention and bringing it under the magnifying glass of our logic — we immediately realize that we cannot be sure of anything at all. And for me, it is of but small comfort that my futile grappling with all these problems shows that I myself "am". That is to say, the question which interests me is not whether I am or am not, but rather the one: "Who am I?" But for this question I find no answer, and I am worried by it, sometimes unbearably. We do not know where we come from, why we were born, and whither we go. Thus, there is enough material for people to think about. But are they really bothered by these questions? Far from it: they care only about wars, money, pleasure, amusement, and games of chance. In this connection I really understand the gambler the best, since the play offers people precisely the gift of forgetting all their worries and fears, at least while they are playing. But is this really good for them? The player ceases to think of himself, the game overpowers him like opium and diverts his attention from the really important questions.[7] Naturally, one is not hurt by plunging from time to time into the bath of which the game offers forgetfulness and refreshment, but nobody should remain there for a long time. I regarded the thinking about the wonderful laws of the games of chance as precisely the means of helping the player to free himself from the magic circle of the game by leading him back to the world of reason and consciousness. In this I see one, if perhaps not the most important, direction and aim of the investigation of mathematical questions about whether and when games of chance are legitimate.

Before turning to the real significance of these problems, let me remark by the way that these investigations in any case had a truly beneficial effect upon the Chevalier de Méré. I met him recently and was rather surprised how much he had changed during the last year. A year ago he was still proud of being a completely disinterested man, an example of *impassibilité*. He heard everything which was said to him with an interest which was polite but not too great, and, indeed, he would have been ashamed to confess that something really interested and fascinated him. He was proud of not being a slave to any passions except the game, and therefore not even to the passion of scientific inquiry. But now he surprised me with his newly gained and well-founded mathematical knowledge and with his serious dealing with different problems. Please do not misunderstand me: I do not pretend that this change is due to me; the germ of this development was hidden ready-made in him before I got to know him. This can be seen clearly from the fact that he independently formulated the problems of dice and he has even found a solution – though a somewhat circumstantial one – for the easier problem.[8] But he could not solve the second one – a problem which was solved by you and by me in entirely different ways and yet with the same result. Perhaps you remember that at that time in my great joy I wrote to you that apparently the truth is the same in Paris and Toulouse.[9] Now as to the change in the Chevalier, I believe that precisely this brought about his change: his pride was hurt because he was unable to find the solution, especially when he became convinced, after understanding ours, that he could have found it himself if he had dealt with it seriously. You naturally know only too well that this is not the case. With every discovery one has a similar impression at the point when he first really understands it. Thus the Chevalier's feeling proves only that he really understood our solution (and indeed I am very glad that he did) and nothing more. But I again digress from my theme, since I wished to speak about the mathematics of chance and not about the remarkable change in the Chevalier de Méré, about whom you are probably not much interested since you do not know him at all.

The oppressive uncertainty, about which I spoke above, has one of its roots partly in a common superstition; namely, if one does not know something with complete certitude (and indeed we are rarely in possession of complete certainty), one is inclined to believe he has no knowledge about it at all. The starting point of my reasoning is the statement that this is an erroneous belief. Partial knowledge is none the less knowledge, and incomplete certainty has a certain value, especially if one is conscious of the degree of certainty of his knowledge. "Why" — somebody could object here — "can one measure the degree of knowledge; how express it by a number?" "Of course", I would answer, "it can be measured and this is exactly what people who play a game of chance are doing". If a gambler throws a die, he cannot know the result of the throw in advance, but he still knows something, namely, that all of the six numbers have the same chance. If we take the whole certainty as a unit, then it follows that a specific one of the numbers 1, 2, 3, 4, 5, 6 will be thrown, manifestly with the degree of certainty of $1/6$. If we in turn throw with one die four times, it is — as it was already observed by the Chevalier de Méré — more advantageous (with equal stakes) to bet on throwing a 6 at least once; this can also be expressed by saying that the degree of certainty in the event that at least one 6 will be thrown in a fourfold dicing is greater than $1/2$. If for an event the chances of occurrence and non-occurrence are equal (as for example, in the case of coin tossing, the chances of a head or a tail coming up), one can say that the degree of certainty of the occurrence of the event is exactly $1/2$. Just as great is the degree of certainty of the non-occurrence of this event. Of course, it is actually arbitrary to assign 1 as the appropriate degree of certainty to the complete certainty; e.g., 100 could have been chosen as well for the degree of certainty belonging to the complete certitude, and then the degree of certainty of a random event (i.e., of an event which does not occur unconditionally) would have been obtained in percentages. As a matter of fact, in every concrete case one could assign any suitably chosen number to complete certainty, e.g., in the case of dicing the number 6; then the degree of certainty of every possible number would be equal to 1. However, I think that the simplest and most natural procedure is always to assign the number 1 to the complete certainty and to measure the degree of certainty of a random event with the fraction giving the event's share of the complete certainty. The degree of certainty of an impossible event is of course equal to zero; thus, if the degree of certainty of a random event is a positive number, then this event is eventually possible, even if its chances may not happen to be very high.

I should like to note here that I have given the degree of certainty of an event the name "probability". I pondered for a long time over the right choice of a term, and finally I chose this one, being as it is the most expressive. Furthermore, this designation is in complete agreement with everyday usage. Of course, in the vernacular we say about a random event only that it is "most probable" or "improbable", or else that one event is more probable than another. I have, however, chosen, as a postulate of my theory, that to every event whose occurrence is not certain but is not excluded either, whose occurrence depends on chance (i.e., to every random event), one can assign a certain number between 0 and 1 as its probability. The probability of an event which is said to be "probable" in everyday language lies near to 1, i.e., near to the probability of complete certainty, while the probabilities of events called "improbable" in common speech are near to 0, i.e., to the probability of an impossible event. As I chose the word "probability", I was somewhat disturbed by the fact that it has an entirely different meaning in casuistry. In the study of casuistry, expressions appearing in the Bible, in papal bulls, or in the canons of the council are "certain", though statements to be found in the books of the doctors of the Church are called only "probable". Thus, when the doctors of the Church are of different, even of contradictory opinions, their statements are said to be "probable".[10] But in my opinion this remarkable usage does not prevent me from employing the word "probable", since I do not believe that anybody will misunderstand it (the Jesuits excepted). Moreover, as to the designation, I am in complete agreement with M. Descartes, who says in his *Règles pour la direction de l'esprit*: "For fear of arousing disgust by using the word 'intuition' as well as other words in a sense distinct from the accustomed one, I call attention to the fact that in what follows I shall avoid completely their ordinary meaning . . . and that in want of proper terms I shall employ metaphorically those words which seem to render my thoughts most conveniently."[11] Similarly, in what follows I shall use the name "probability" to denote the degree of certainty.

The essence of the previous discussion is the insight that incomplete knowledge can have its value too, but only if we know its degree of certainty. Thus, if we know numerically the probability of a random (i.e., uncertain) event, we know something concrete and definite about it. Partial certainty should therefore be valued, but not overvalued, nor should it be mistaken for complete certainty. This fact was expressed most succinctly by Montaigne, whose *Essays* (though I often quarrel with them inwardly) mean more to me than any other book: "I have an aversion even against the most probable propositions, if they are stated as certain."[12] Here Montaigne speaks to my heart! It has often happened that my friends have tried to convince me about something with which, by and large, I indeed believed I agreed, even if not completely. But they wanted to force me to accept their viewpoint without any conditions. The conclusion of the discussion was always that, at its end, our views were far more divergent and apart than they were at the beginning. Thus it appeared that we differed even in questions in which we believed ourselves to be of the same opinion, and we parted as men of entirely different ideas. I think Montaigne must have had similar experiences, since these are necessarily produced by similar circumstances in men whose words coincide with their deeds — *quibus vivere est cogitare*.[13] But I have digressed once again; actually I did not wish to speak about Montaigne, and referred to him only in order to show that, although the idea to measure probability numerically is a new one, still it is a logical development of earlier well-known thoughts.

Certainly you must have already perceived that in measuring the degree of certainty I started from the implicit assumption that complete certainty is unrestrictedly divisible, just like line, space, or number. But can the probability of a random event really take up every value between 0 and 1? This is a question worth study, and I shall demonstrate it by a simple example.

My friends smile at my habit — certainly unique in Paris, though one I find quite natural — of always carrying a watch in my pocket and every night putting it beside my bed so that if I awake (which occurs, alas, too often) I will know the time. Now my question is: How large is the probability that, when I awake and consult my watch, the minute hand will show, for example, a value between 15 and 20 minutes? Since the minute hand moves uniformly and there are just 5 minutes of the 60 (i.e., 1/12 of every hour) between the above-said limits, the probability looked for is $5/60 = 1/12$. The same result will be obtained, if one considers that the direction of the minute hand, to satisfy the desired condition, must lie within an angle of 30°;

so the probability looked for is $30°/360° = 1/12$. But if I choose such an angle on my watch of the magnitude $360° x$, where x is an arbitrary number between 0 and 1, then, when I awake and consult my watch, the probability that I shall find the minute hand within the chosen angle is exactly equal to x.

In the case of games of chance, of course, only probabilities occur which can be expressed as quotients of whole numbers; since games of chance have always a finite number of equally possible, mutually exclusive outcomes, the probability of each event is equal to the number of the outcomes favorable for this event, divided by the number of all outcomes. Thus, for instance, in dicing with a single die there are six outcomes (one throws 1, 2, 3, 4, 5, or 6) and thus the probability of the event that a 6 will be thrown is equal to 1/6, and the probability of the event that no 6 will be thrown is equal to 5/6 (since the number of the favorable outcomes is in the first case 1 and in the second 5). Thus the sum of the probabilities of the events that one throws a 6 and that one does not throw a 6 is equal to 1. This holds obviously for any event, since the probability of the certain event, that is 1, is distributed between an event and its opposite. More generally, if an event can occur in several mutually exclusive ways, then its probability is equal to the sum of the probabilities of its different possible occurrences, just as in the distribution of a certain amount of fluid into several vessels, the sum of the amounts of fluid in the individual vessels remains equal to the whole amount of fluid. In other words, if in a play we consider several mutually exclusive events, the sum of the probabilities of these events is equal to the probability of the occurrence of any one of these events. This rule I shall call the *rule of addition of the probabilities.*

Beside this almost obvious rule, I have stated another, deeper one, which I shall call the *multiplication rule of probabilities,* as follows: If one plays a game two times, the probability that a certain event occurs in the first game and a certain event (which can be identical with or different from the first) occurs in the second game is equal to the product of the probabilities of these events in the individual games. Thus, for instance, if I throw the die twice, the probability that I obtain on both the first and second throws a number different from 6 is equal to $5/6.5/6 = 25/36$. That is to say, the result of the double throw can be any ordered number pair formed from the numbers 1, 2, . . . 6, and there are but 36 such number pairs, and among these, there are 25 both of whose members are distinct from 6. Similarly, if I throw four times with a die, the probability of throwing no 6 at all is equal to 25/36.25/36 = 625/1296, since in this case I must not throw the 6 on the first two, or on the second two throws, either. Hence the probability of the opposite event, i.e., of the event that among the four throws a 6 will occur at least once, is equal to 1–625/1296 = 671/1296. Thus we obtain the answer, well known to you, of the first question of the Chevalier de Méré.

Thus the first two basic laws of the mathematics of chance are so simple! You wonder, perhaps, if we are dealing here with mathematics at all, or with a science in which some mathematical considerations are applied. I am of the opinion that here there is a new branch of mathematics which may be called the mathematics of chance (as I did in my letter to the Parisian Academy); indeed, one could also speak of a *calculus of probabilities*; I find this second name still more expressive.

Let us then baptize the new doctrine, which has as its aim to state something definite about what is random, what is uncertain, and let us give it the name: calculus of probabilities! The answer to the question of whether the calculus of probabilities is indeed a branch of mathematics depends of course on our interpretation of mathematics as a whole. If by mathematics one understands its traditional capital stock only, geometry, arithmetic, and algebra, there is naturally in this narrow definition no room for any new branch. I agree in this respect with Descartes, however, according to whom[14] every study, having for its aim the investigation of measure and order, belongs to mathematics irrespective of the object whose measure and order it investigates.

Now that I have put all of this down on paper, I feel a certain relief (since the difficulties of formulation are behind me) and, at the same time, an intensive anguish (since I do not know if I have succeeded in expressing the ideas seething in me). Please be so kind as to free me from this double mood by sending me your opinion about my newly born child christened "calculus of probabilities". If you find some lack, error, or contradiction in my reasoning, please tell me without any reservation or forbearance. You may be sure that I will gratefully accept from you even the most severe criticism.

For the time being I have put aside many important questions which have been occupying my mind for a long time. If your answer assures me that I am on the right road, then I shall organize my further thoughts about the subject and entrust them to you. Probably you will spare me this trouble through your answer, where my own ideas will be expressed in a perfect form which I myself would be incapable of giving them. That is, I cannot finish this letter (grown rather long) without confessing that, as I pondered over the questions dealt with above, I reread your letters on dicing more than once and tried, by reading between the lines, to guess your hidden thoughts. While thinking over these problems, I discussed them with you in my imagination and much of what I have written down are answers to questions which you put to me in this imaginary discussion. I would be happy if it turned out that this was not a mere fancy of my mind, but that the things presented above were really your thoughts, which have been reconstructed – if roughly and inadequately – by your sincere and loyal adherent and admirer,

Blaise Pascal

Paris, November 6, 1654

M. Pierre Fermat
Orléans

Sir,

Letters have never given me so much pleasure as that of yours sent to me through M. de Carcavi. I awaited impatiently for his return so that I might ask him how my letter of October 28 was received. At the same time I hoped he would bring me your promise of an answer in the near future. But that he brought the answer itself indeed surpassed my boldest hopes. Therefore I hasten to answer promptly, though your letter contains material for thought covering months, and thus my prompt answer must necessarily be an incomplete one. As I have observed, some players of chess restrict the time of thinking and control the play by means of an hourglass. Our correspondence is indeed like such a chess party in which I am glad to partake without bothering myself that in this contest only you can be the winner.

And thus, I shall try to answer your questions. To do this as promptly as I do now — you must decide whether rightly or wrongly — was only made possible by my previous lengthy musings upon the same questions, which thus found me in a mood that is quite far from being unprepared. In fact, as I sealed my preceding letter, I was aware that I should have dealt with these questions — especially with your second question — in that first letter. But so it is with me always; when I write something, only at the end do I recognize how I should have begun it. But just because I know my work habits and am never satisfied with the beginning of a piece of writing at the moment when I put a period at its end, I did not change my letter and sent it to you as it was; if I had rewritten it, I would again have been dissatisfied.

Your first question is rather easy to answer and I am indeed convinced that the answer is already well-known to you; I suppose you only wished to test me to find out how carefully I had pondered the subject? In fact, about your question concerning my demonstration that the probability of an event can be calculated by dividing the number of the outcomes favorable for the event in question by the number of all equally possible and mutually exclusive outcomes, you are perfectly right that I could have said "equally probable" outcomes instead of "equally possible" outcomes, since the meaning of these two expressions is the same. You ask if a kind of a *circulus vitiosus* does not lurk behind this identity, for the definition of the probability seems to depend on the concept of "equally probable events" so that we defined probability by itself, which is of course forbidden and as absurd as if somebody said he could lift himself by his own hair.

Actually, however, there is no logical error here, since we have to deal not with the definition of probability as a concept, but rather with a rule for determining the numerical values of certain probabilities. According to my assumption, every random event has a certain probability which is a number between 0 and 1 and indicates the degree of the incomplete certainty of the event in question. The question of whether or not two events are equally probable can be decided without knowing the numerical values of these probabilities. If I say that a die is regular, this means that its faces, if they were not numbered, would not be distinguishable from each other at all. If somebody in my absence provides the faces with a new numeration, I cannot perceive this manipulation at all. This much is clear: the die falls with the same probability upon each one of its six faces. This situation is similar to the procedure of the direct comparing of two segments, when one decides immediately without measuring them and by putting one on the other whether they are equal or not. Similarly, one can decide if two objects have the same weight by balancing them without actually weighing them.

The answer to your second question is much more difficult. That is, you ask, How can one determine the probabilities of the individual faces in the case of a false die (to continue the example) having a center of gravity which does not coincide with its geometrical center? This question, which seems at first glance to be trivial, is actually a very deep one and in order to answer it, we have first to clear another fundamental problem which, strictly speaking, ought to have been dealt with in my first letter. Of course, if you were to put this question to my friend, the Chevalier de Méré, he would try to avoid the answer by saying that he gambles with honorable people only and in a society where anyone who proves himself to use false dice would be thrown out, together with his dice. Now of course you could rightfully ask him how he can show the falsity of a die. And now the Chevalier would have only one answer: when the number of 6's thrown with a false die is greater than what is expected when thrown with a regular one, because just this greater frequency is the aim of the falsification. Thus, if you were further to ask logically — I hope you will pardon me this fictive dialogue with you as a protagonist — what result the Chevalier would expect with a regular die, then of course he would answer that in a game lasting long enough, the 6 should occur approximately with the same frequency as all the other numbers, i.e., it would amount to approximately 1/6 of all throws. Herewith, however, the Chevalier would have answered your original question, too. In fact, if with a false die one throws the 6 approximately $x N$ times in N throws, where x is a number greater than 1/6, then clearly the probability of throwing the 6 with this false die is equal to x. But you could now put a more delicate question, namely, if one had thrown the 6 with a false die, e.g., 150 times in 600 throws, does this mean that the probability of throwing the 6 with this die is *exactly* equal to $150/600 = 1/4$? The Chevalier (assuming he has read my previous letter and would use the expressions introduced in it) could now answer that this would be a somewhat hurried conclusion since even if the die were perfectly regular and the probability of throwing the 6 were exactly equal to 1/6, one would not be able to state that the 6 will be thrown exactly 100 times in 600 throws, only that it will occur *approximately* 100 times. Consequently, the result of an experiment with our false die does not mean that the probability of throwing the six with it is exactly equal to 1/4, but only that it is nearly equal to 1/4. You now could continue to ask him how, in spite of this, one could determine the exact value of the probability looked for. The Chevalier, as a skilled gambler, would obviously answer that he does not know any method for the exact determination of the probability in question and that a better and more reliable approximation can be obtained by raising the number of the throws — e.g., to 1200, if you happen to be dissatisfied with the degree of approximation — though the mentioned experiment as regards the falsity of the die is quite convincing and this die would be immediately tossed into the fire. For instance, if in a series of 1200 throws, the 6 occurs 288 times, a more reliable approximation of the probability in question will be 288/1200 = 0.24. Perhaps the Chevalier would add (since, as I have already mentioned, he is lately much interested in philosophy) that though a die may be regular in one way, still it can be irregular in infinitely many other ways, just like the number of all possible lies, which is infinite.

I shall not continue this fictive dialogue since you could not learn much more from the Chevalier — and you know all of this anyhow. Instead, I should like to try to answer your question in my own words.

To be concise I should like to introduce some definitions. If we repeat an experiment several times under the same circumstances, then the number of the experiments in which a certain event E occurs will be called the *frequency* of the event E, and the quotient of the frequency of the event E and the number of all experiments (in which we observe the occurrence or the non-occurrence of E) will be called the *relative frequency* of E with respect to the given sequence of experiments. Anyone who has some experience in gambling knows that the relative frequency of an arbitrary event in a game within a long sequence in general approximates a definite number which has been called the probability of this event, and the divergence of the relative frequency from the probability is less the longer the game is played. Thus, for instance, in dicing the relative frequency of the 6 for 100 throws will lie near the probability of the 6, that is, near 1/6 if the die is regular, and near to some other number if it is false. This, even for the false die, is the only way approximately to determine the probabilities of the individual faces. In principle, by this empirical method one can approximate the probabilities with an arbitrary precision; in practice, of course, the precision cannot be increased without restriction — it would take a very long time, and, apart from everything else, the die itself would be entirely worn out by use during the continuous tossing. I believe, however, that you are not really interested in the exact numerical value of the probability of throwing the 6 with a false die, but rather in the question of how one can determine the probability of a random event at all, if the problem cannot be reduced to the counting of the favorable cases among the equally probable outcomes of an experiment. This rule which we can apply with respect to the regular (but not to the irregular) die can be called symmetry consideration, since it rests upon the symmetrical properties of the regular die. The example of the crystals shows that symmetry occurs not only among man-made objects but in nature as well. There are natural phenomena completely devoid of symmetry, however. If we observe the shingles on the shore polished by the sea, we can scarcely find a single one of a regular shape, e.g., of a sphere. Man himself is not completely symmetrical, either. Lately I have read somewhere that in the Roman Empire the soldiers played not with regular wooden or ivory dice (these — the Tessera — were used only by the rich) but with the so-called talus or taxillus: that is, with the heelbone and kneebone of the goat or sheep. These osselots, the so-called astragali, were used in ancient Greece for the same purpose. The probabilities of the different possible throws for these osselots can be approximately determined only empirically, through the observation of relative frequencies.

The taxillus too has six sides, but of these two are rounded, and thus it can stand only in four different positions. The Greeks and Romans tossed four osselots simultaneously. The best of all throws was considered that in which each of the four showed a different side. This throw was called the "venus". I recently procured two osselots something like these old ones and performed a few experiments with them. With one, the frequencies of the four sides among 1000 throws were equal to 408, 396, 91, and 105. I tossed the other only 100 times and then I lost it somehow. Within the 100 throws I observed the frequencies 38, 48, 11, and 8. Let us call the two most probable falls of the taxillus A and B, the two less probable falls, C and D. For the sake of simplicity let us assume that the probabilities of A and B are both equal to 4/10 and those of C and D equal to 1/10. According to my experiments this assumption is approximately correct. In this case — you can calculate it yourself — the probability of throwing a venus with four astragali is equal to 24/625. That is, according to the multiplication rule mentioned in my previous letter, we must first of all form the product of the four probabilities which is 4/10.4/10.1/10.1/10 = 11/625; this gives the probability that in a certain arrangement the four astragali show in turn the sides A, B, C, D; since, however, four letters can be arranged in 24 possible ways, 24 mutually exclusive distinct arrangements are possible for the realization of a "venus". Thus, by applying the rule of addition, we obtain that the probability of the "venus" is equal to 24/625, that is, somewhat smaller than 1/25. Thus it is clear why the Romans considered a person lucky who happened to throw a "venus".

Naturally, taxillus bones are never completely uniform and thus it is possible that the probability of side A for different samples is not the same; e.g., it is 0.4 for one item, 0.38 for the other, and so on. But if we select one taxillus, then the probability of throwing A with it is a definite number. Nevertheless, the relative frequency of an A throw with a given taxillus-osselot in a large sequence of experiments of a prescribed length is still to a certain degree uncertain, depending as it does on chance; the only sure thing is that it will lie in the neighborhood of probability. Thus, for instance, if we perform 100 throws with a taxillus which has for its side A the probability 0.4, it is not at all certain that we shall throw the A exactly 40 times; this number can also be 39 or 41, 44 or 36, etc.; if we perform in turn several sequences of 100 throws, the frequency and thus the relative frequency of an A throw will in general be different in the individual sequences, but almost always it will be near the probability, i.e., to 0.4. Thus the probability of an event is the fixed point around which the relative frequency of the event fluctuates in an unpredictable manner, but from which it deviates at most only a little during all these capricious fluctuations. If we increase the number of observations, the deviations of the frequency from the expected value (i.e., from the product of the number of all observations and the probability) will in general also be somewhat greater, but the deviation of the relative frequency from the probability will mostly decrease. Thus, for instance, when we perform with a taxillus sequences of 400 throws, the frequency of the C throws will deviate from the expected value (i.e., from $400.1/10 = 40$) mostly less than by around 12; if, however, we perform sequences of 1000 throws, the frequency of the C throws will deviate from the expected value (i.e., from $1000.1/10 = 100$) quite often by around 12 or even more, but rarely more than 20. But this means that the relative frequency of C throws in sequences of 400 throws will lie mostly between 7/100 and 13/100 but, in sequences of 1000 throws, mostly between the narrower limits of 8/100 and 12/100.

Thus, while the probability of a random event is a definite (though to us perhaps not exactly known) number which does not depend on chance, the frequency of an event is an uncertain, chance-dependent number, the exact value of which cannot be determined in advance. Although the value of the relative frequency is known to us through observation, we must not forget that this value could have been a different one too, and that in any repetition of the experiment we must take into account the possibility of finding another number. If we know the probability (e.g., if we have determined it from symmetry considerations and, eventually, from the application of the rules of addition and multiplication, or of some other similar rules), then we can foresee more or less exactly the value of relative frequency; on the other hand, from the observation of the relative frequency we can conclude the value of the probability — if this is unknown — with more or less precision. These two kinds of conclusion differ fundamentally, however. As to the first, it can be compared to the calculation of the mass of an object from its known density and known volume; the second, however, is something like calculating the unknown density of some material from its mass and from the volume of an object consisting of the material in question. Generally, the values obtained for the density will not be exactly the same, but only somewhat adjacent to one another, since every measurement is burdened with error.

Thus probability and relative frequency are in the same relation to each other as the exact value of the density of its value calculated from measurements, and the observation of the relative frequency can be considered as a measuring procedure for the measurement of probability. This measuring procedure (like every measuring method) provides only an inexact value, but the inexactness of the measurement can be decreased at will by increasing the number of observations. But this is not the method for determining the probability with absolute exactness. Montaigne once made the remark[15] that we can never obtain complete certainty from facts, since facts are always changing. We can complete this assertion of Montaigne as follows: not even the degree of certainty can be determined exactly from mere facts. In practice, we must be satisfied with incomplete knowledge of the degree of certainty. By way of comparison, you are thus in a situation as if you had obtained only a part of my letter, the rest being lost on the way, and even this part being only incompletely readable because of the carelessness of the postilion who let it fall into the mud. Let us hope that my letter is not destined to a fate like this; but with documents from old times, such damages are almost always unavoidable. Nevertheless, history can still recover something, though our knowledge of the past is always to a certain degree hypothetical, even if most historians do not like to acknowledge it.

To sum up, we can ascertain that, approximately, the frequency of an event is to the number of all observations as the probability of the event is to the probability of the certainty, i.e., to 1. I find this correspondence between facts and logic, between possibility and realization, wonderful indeed!

The two kinds of conclusions can also be applied in another way: from the observation of the frequencies we can conclude the value of certain probabilities, other probabilities can again be calculated by means of the rules of the probability theory, and from these we can infer the occurrence of events in the future. Thus observation and thinking, mutually completing and helping each other, make knowledge of the world possible. But I am far from pretending that I am the first to discover this; I am convinced that Plato, for instance, was perfectly aware of it. Not long ago I reread *Timaeus* and found the following surprising sentence[16] in it: "As Being is to Becoming, even so is Truth to Opinion." I am convinced that Plato by this somewhat enigmatical sentence wished to express precisely the ideas discussed above. My conviction is based upon the text in which, just after the above-cited sentence, Timaeus speaks about things which are not sure but merely probable. It seems to me that in Greece there lived certain other philosophers — Carneades, for instance — who understood this sentence of Plato, but that, since then, its real meaning has been lost to oblivion. When some days ago I found this passage in *Timaeus*, I felt like somebody who had unearthed a beautiful Greek statue and, after cleaning the mud from it, saw the marble glisten with its old luster.

My candle is now only a mere stub, and thus I realize how long I have dwelt upon the answer to your second question. Your third question is simpler to answer, though this, too, like a torch shines into the parts of our topic which still remain in darkness. I hope you will pardon me, however, if I postpone the answer, since early tomorrow morning I shall give this letter to a reliable person, who is immediately starting out for Orléans, where you — as I have heard from M. de Carcavi — are to be found at present.

I am most anxious that you receive this letter as soon as possible in order to see how the seeds you have sown have brought forth fruit in such a short time. I hope you will find these fruits — though they are not as yet perfectly ripe — rather enjoyable. But because I am afraid that these fruits are somewhat tart, I am also sending you a basket of apples from my garden. I am perfectly aware that these apples are not better than those which grow in Toulouse; nevertheless, this humble gift may help convince you that nobody can esteem you more sincerely and fervently than

Your

Blaise Pascal

Paris, November 8, 1654,
                                           early in the morning

                                           To M. Pierre Fermat
                                           Orléans

Sir,

Last night I had a very strange dream from which I awoke in a
sweat and with a throbbing heart. To divert my thoughts from this
dream I decided to answer your third question, namely, under what
conditions is the multiplication rule of the calculus of probabilities
valid? You have particularly objected that in the case of drawing
two cards in turn from a pack, the validity of the multiplication rule
depends on whether the card drawn first was replaced before the
second drawing and the pack thoroughly shuffled, or whether the
card was not replaced at all.

If the pack consists of 16 cards and contains of each of the suits
(spade, heart, club, and diamond) the ace, king, queen, and jack,
then the probability of drawing a king at the first draw is equal
to $1/4$. The probability of drawing a king at the second draw is also
$1/4$ and, furthermore — as we shall see later — it does not depend on
whether the card was or was not replaced before the second drawing.
If we do not replace the card drawn for the first time, the probability
of drawing a king both times is not equal to $1/4.1/4 = 1/16$, but only
equal to $1/20$, since two kings in succession can be drawn in $4.3 = 12$
different ways and the number of all possibilities is $16/15 = 240$.
Indeed, one has the impression that this would be in contradiction
to my multiplication rule mentioned in my letter of October 28; but
this is only an apparent contradiction. As soon as we investigate this
example more closely, it will appear that the multiplication rule is
valid in this case also.

If one draws first a king and does not replace it to the pack before
the second drawing, there are only 15 cards in the pack and among
them only three kings. Thus the probability of again drawing a king
the second time is equal to $3/15 = 1/5$; since, however, $1/4.1/5 = 1/20$
applies, the rule of multiplication holds in this case as well. On the
assumption that at the first drawing not a king but some other card
is drawn, and is not replaced, the probability of drawing a king the

second time is equal to 4/15. Hence, by means of the multiplication rule 3/4.4/15 = 1/5, we hold as a probability that no king will be drawn the first time, but a king will be drawn the second. Thus probability of drawing a king the second time, since the result of the first drawing can be either a king or no king, is equal to 1/20 + 1/5 = 1/4 — hence, the same as if the card drawn for the first time had been put back before the second drawing. This reasoning, however, holds only if the card drawn for the first time was not inspected. But if we look at the card and realize that it is a king, the probability of drawing a king the second time is merely 1/5 (thus less than 1/4), while in the case that the card drawn for the first time is not a king, this probability is equal to 4/15 (thus greater than 1/4). The question, of course, is how can the probability depend on looking at the card drawn for the first time? Surely, the card cannot know whether this was or was not done! In other words, how can my knowledge influence the probability of the second drawing, depending as it does only on the composition of the pack of cards? This, of course, is so, but when I inspect the card drawn for the first time, I realize only the fact that one of the 16 cards is not among the 15, and the fact of this card's not being there affects the probability in question, since this depends on the number of the kings among the 15 cards, which is either four or three. Basically, it is indeed somewhat misleading to say that we "inspect" the drawn card, since whether we realize that the card drawn for the first time is or is not a king does not matter; it is only the fact itself that matters. If we are interested only in the card drawn for the second time, then in order to calculate the probability of drawing a king the second time we must consider both possibilities of the first drawing, i.e., that a king or some other card is drawn, and we have to form the *weighted mean* of the conditional probabilities 1/5 and 4/15, where the weights are the two possible results of the first drawing, i.e., 1/3 and 3/4. Thus we obtain indeed 1/4.1/5 + 3/4.4/15 = 1/20 + 1/5 = 1/4.

This example shows how much precaution is needed, even in dealing with a seemingly very simple problem, since at almost every step traps are lurking. I should like to write you more about this later, but now back to the question of the multiplication rule. This rule can be explained in a general and correct form as follows: The probability that the events A and B both occur is equal to the product of the probability of event A and the probability of event B, where the latter probability must be computed under the condition that the occurrence of the event A is a completed fact. I shall call this latter value the "conditional probability" of the event B with respect to the condition A.

It seems as if I had introduced a new concept here, namely, that of the conditional probability. This concept, however, does not differ basically from that of the simple probability. The probability of any event depends on conditions with respect to which its occurrence or non-occurrence is observed. Thus, for instance, when we ascertain that the probability of throwing the 6 with a die is equal to 1/6, we moreover assume implicitly that the die is a regular one. When we say that the probability of drawing a king from a pack of cards is equal to 1/4, we assume that the pack consists of 16 cards, including four kings, that it is thoroughly shuffled, and that the drawer sees only the backside of the cards. If the conditions change, the probability, in general, changes too. On the whole, therefore, probabilities are all conditional; when the conditions are well known and unchanging, they are not mentioned at all. But if the conditions change, this must be considered as well. Thus the expression "conditional probability" is actually a pleonasm, just like the expression "a mortal man", since it is known that every man is mortal. Still in order to avoid misunderstandings, it is always expedient to speak about conditional probabilities if the conditions are changing.

It can happen, however, that the probability of the event B with respect to the condition that the event A occurred is equal to the probability of the event B without this condition. In this case it is justifiable to call the events A and B "independent", since the probability of B does not depend on the occurrence or non-occurrence of A, yes, not even on whether the occurrence or non-occurrence of A was considered or was not. If events A and B are independent, the multiplication rule can be formulated for them without the use of the concept of conditional probability; in cases like this one can ascertain without much ado that the probability of the occurrence of both A and B is equal to the product of the probabilities of the individual events. This is the case, for example, when the events A and B refer to throwing the dice with two different dice. Then events A and B are clearly independent since the two dice are unable to affect each other. If the dice were somehow connected, for instance by a string, then these two events would not be independent. But in order for two events to be independent, it is not absolutely necessary that one should not be able to imagine how the occurrence of the one event could influence the chances of the other. For instance, let A denote the event that a card drawn from the above-mentioned pack of cards is a spade and let B denote that this card is a king. In this case, both events refer to the same drawing and they are still independent; since among the 16 cards there are four kings, while among the four cards of the suit spade there is one king; among the 12 other cards there are three kings; hence the probability of the event that B is equal to 1/4, and both are under the condition that A occurs and also under the condition that A does not occur; finally, it is the same even if the event A is not considered at all.

November 8, evening

Now that I have reread what I wrote early this morning, I can see that my answer brings up new questions. I pondered what it actually means that a pack of cards is "thoroughly shuffled". If I asked an experienced player what it means — for instance, the Chevalier de Méré — his answer certainly would be that this means somebody has shuffled the pack of cards for a sufficiently long time without the intention of any swindle, that is, he has often performed the usual shuffling movements according to the relevant prescriptions and thus he has created the possibility of a random arrangement of the cards. But may I ask further if one could ascertain from the mere arrangement of the cards (without knowing how they have been shuffled) whether or not they have been thoroughly shuffled at all? At first sight one does not see what an insidious question this in reality is. I wonder, indeed, what the Chevalier de Méré would answer. For after his proposition for the proof of a thorough shuffling, I could ask him how large is the probability that after such a shuffling the queen of hearts, or any other card, would be the top card? Obviously, he would have to answer that, after a thorough shuffling, each of the 16 cards would have the same probability for being on the top, thus the probability 1/16. If the queen of hearts is on the top — I would ask further — how large is the probability, for instance, that the ace of spades would be the next to the top card. The probability is, of course, 1/15 — which would be the answer. The continuation of the same reasoning leads to the recognition that after a thorough shuffling each of the possible arrangements must have the same probability. But if this is so, how can one decide, upon the basis of the arrangement of the cards, that they were indeed thoroughly shuffled? Since we can take any one of the arrangements, none of them is more or less probable than any other possible arrangement. But if one cannot decide from the arrangement of the cards whether the pack was or was not thoroughly shuffled, what is then the precise sense of this statement? To this the Chevalier could answer that one really cannot decide by means of a single shuffle whether the mixer swindles or does not, but if he deals himself an advantageous hand more often than it could be expected in advance, this would be a proof that he swindles. But I would ask the Chevalier again if he thinks, provided an honest shuffler were at work, every possible arrangement would occur equally often. And if the unsuspicious Chevalier answers yes to the question, he has already fallen into my trap, because the number of all possible arrangements of 16 cards is equal to the product of the first 16 positive whole numbers, and this is such an enormously large number that somebody shuffling the cards day and night without interruption and allowing no more than one minute shuffling would have to shuffle the cards for 39 million years so that every arrangement should occur at least once. In practice, therefore, the thoroughness of the shuffling cannot be proved in this way. I imagined a simple machine for shuffling the cards: the cards fall along an oblique plane into a box; then a clockwork raises the box and pours the cards again upon the oblique plane where they slide down again, and so on. With such a machine one could shuffle the cards perhaps about ten times a minute, but even so it would take some 4 million years before all possible arrangements could occur. And then, as I wished to calculate how many arrangements are possible with 52 cards, I began to feel dizzy.

Let us forget for a minute the delicate question of how the thoroughness of the shuffling can be proved, and let us suppose that we have a reliable machine (or an experienced and reliable gambler) able to produce all possible arrangements with the same probability. Now the machine (or the player) shuffles the 16 cards, and one of the more than 20 billion arrangements is realized. Please imagine for yourself what this means: before our eyes there occurs an event having a probability which is less than 0.00000000000005! Before realizing this, I was convinced that it is practically impossible for an event

34

with a very small probability really to occur. However, as the example of the shuffling of the cards shows, one has to deal more carefully with such statements. After all, in what sense is it, then, still true that the occurrence of events with a very small probability can be considered as practically impossible and, similarly, the occurrence of events with a probability near to 1 as practically sure? I think the question is not as difficult as it seemed to me at first because when I choose a definite arrangement in advance and I write it down and, after doing this, I shuffle the cards, then it is indeed practically impossible to obtain the same arrangement again, though it is by no means less probable than the one actually occurring as the result of the shuffling.

When I began to muse about probability, everything first seemed to be so simple and clear, and only now do I realize how wrong I was! Every time I believe I have grasped the truth, it again slips out of my hands. There are lurking abysses at almost every step of the way. Perhaps my dream, which agitated me so much last night, mirrors just this kind of anxiety. I dreamed that I was in a cave and looked for the way out by groping about in the darkness. I tried to move in the direction of a glimmering light. The way was blocked by a large rock, but finally I succeeded in circumventing it and saw an opening that obviously led out from the cave. I rose and made one step in the direction of the opening. Then I suddenly had the feeling of being seized by the shoulders and being thrown back. Evidently my shoulder was knocked against a protrusion of the rock – thought I; since I was aware that no one but myself was in the cave, I tried again to approach the supposed way out, but now I was more careful and groped about along the walls and looked for the way with my feet. Suddenly I shrank back: before my feet yawned a dark abyss! Had something or somebody not thrust me back a short while ago, I would have unavoidably fallen into it. At first I did not at all realize from what a danger I had been saved. Then out of curiosity I threw a stone into the gaping void and began to count in order to calculate the depth of the abyss by means of the time spanned until I heard the crack of the stone at the bottom of the abyss. I counted to five and still did not hear anything and I began to understand the situation; trembling, I counted to ten, to twenty, but still I did not hear anything at all! I continued counting with chattering teeth – till I finally awakened.

I believe it is understandable that after this I could not fall asleep again and began to write at early dawn to free myself from the depressing memory of my dreams.

Now I am able again to ponder calmly over my dream, but I do not know what to think about it. Was it simply my wrestling with the mysterious concept of probability which is always slipping out of my hands, which was precipitated in the form of a vision in my dream, as described by Lucretius:[17] "And whatever be the pursuit to which one clings with devotion, whatever the things on which we have been occupied much in the past, the mind being thus more intent upon that pursuit, it is generally the same thing that we seem to encounter in dreams"; or has the dream another meaning? What kind of dangers are lurking around me and what unknown hand has saved me from perishing? Where do our dreams actually come from and have they any meaning at all? My common sense suggests that in dreams my mind at rest is mixing the images stored in it, like a player who shuffles cards, and thus every arrangement of these images can occur by chance; therefore, it would be as vain to look for any mysterious meaning in this order as in the case of the arrangements of the cards. The notion of chance was for thousands of years surrounded by superstitious imaginations which hindered its scientific investigation. I believe that concerning chance I succeeded in freeing it from the paralyzing shackles of superstitious horror; but, concerning my dream, I cannot get rid of the feeling that it must somehow be interpretable, though this feeling cannot be strengthened by any logically valid argument.

Please excuse me that now I further bother you with the description of my dream. On one hand, I am a little ashamed of it, but on the other, it relieves me to communicate sincerely to you my anxieties about this dream. I hope that you, who know my thoughts so well, will understand — even if with some shaking of the head — my present mood as well. Certainly, this would alienate me from everybody else to whom I am not connected by such a spiritual bond as to you, but you — as I hope — will consider my sincerity a proof of my affection and will see from this letter, too, how much you are revered, and how much the honor brought to him by your friendship is appreciated by

Your

Blaise Pascal

Paris, Thursday, November 19, 1654

To M. Pierre Fermat
Toulouse

Sir,

In your letter written in Orléans on November 12, you say with great modesty that my guess about your knowing in advance the answers to your questions does not hold. Please do not be angry if I still persist in my opinion that my answer could not have contained much novelty for you. It is just because I am convinced that you have already answered your own questions that I am so glad to see your agreement — in essence — with my answers.

With respect to the new questions put in your last letter, I am more inclined to believe that they are indeed not merely rhetorical. These questions are so inseparably connected to the fundamental problems of philosophy that they must repeatedly be put by each thinker of every age. Though the development of the sciences opens the way to more and more complete answers to these questions, to give a final answer to them will scarcely ever be possible. It is, however, to your credit that you put these questions in an exceptionally clear form.

If I were to awake after three hundred years and see that mathematicians, scientists, and philosophers are still wrangling about your questions, indeed, I would not be surprised at all. And I would not be astonished, either, if those future philosophers were even then expressing many unclear and confused opinions in their discussions. Because uncertainty is dealt with, it could be rightly expected that superficial minds would be of the opinion that in this domain of problems one can disregard complete clarity of thinking. It would not surprise me if people, to whom exact mathematical reasoning is altogether foreign, believed since random events can never be known with an absolute certainty and can only be foreseen in rough outlines, that they had the right to a certain nonchalance in dealing with the mathematical investigation of chance and allowed themselves to toss out concepts half thought through and indigestible. But the case is just the opposite. Every housewife knows that the sharpness of the knife's edge is of much more importance if the bread to be cut is fresh than if it is dry. Exactly so, every science must approximate truth with the edge of objectivity, with sharp logic, with clear reasoning, every step being carefully controlled. And this is nowhere of greater importance than in the investigation of the laws of chance.

Therefore you will not be surprised if I make no attempt at all to give a final and, in every respect, complete answer to your question. Nevertheless, I shall hasten to write down everything I can say about the problem, if for no other reason than to show you how much I was occupied and how much my thoughts were moved by your writing. I am doing this with more pleasure, since your questions were not entirely unexpected by me. I have been engaged in these problems for some time past, although I could not formulate them as sharply as you have been able to.

Lately, in Madame d'Aiguillon's salon I conducted before a large group a long discussion about this problem with my old friend M. Damien Miton, who, by the way, was present at the occasion when the Chevalier de Méré put his questions to me about dicing. Since then M. Miton has become interested in these things, of course, after his own manner, and asks me, from time to time, how far in the meantime I have progressed in the mathematics of chance. You must know that M. Miton, although no mathematician, is a man of high culture and razor-sharp intelligence, who is interested not only in literature – which he knows well and studies carefully – but also in science. He has a characteristic which often stimulates me to contradiction: namely, to have firm opinions, even in cases in which he has heard nothing about the subjects in question before the discussion. It is just this self-confidence which irritates me and I often try to prove to him that his opinion has been formed hurriedly. You can imagine him for yourself if I tell you how a dispute ends in cases where he is already pressed so hard that he actually ought to confess his failure. M. Miton then says that although he acknowledges the validity of an opinion fundamentally different from his and that he does not wish to force his opinion upon me, but gladly acknowledges that I have the same right to my point of view as he to his, but that he requests that I do not force my opinion upon him, either. His favorite phrase is: "Some prefer blondes, others brunettes" – and he always adds that, as far as he is concerned, he has in this respect no prejudice at all. Herewith the dispute is mostly finished and the discussion turns to beautiful women – a theme on which I have never had any doubts with respect to the deep knowledge and well-founded judgment of M. Miton. With this I think that I have introduced to you M. Miton with all his virtues and weaknesses. After all, his main point of view is that everybody has the same right to form his own opinion, and nobody has the right to restrict others in their assertion of this freedom; we can learn from history that men like him have brought far less trouble, suffering, and horror upon humanity than those who, by fire and sword, inquisition and funeral pyres, wished to enforce their own – real or imagined – truths upon people. In the light of the events of the past hundred years, I am not astonished at all that nowadays so many people think like Monsieur Miton. And as to science, freedom is its life-giving breath, without which it is doomed to suffocate. In spite of all this, I cannot agree with Monsieur Miton. In science, certainly, free opinion must never deteriorate into a "freedom" which disregards facts. If an opinion contradicts the facts, or if it is simply senseless, or inconsistent and even logically false, then it is simply stupid to uphold such an opinion. Moreover, scientific development would be finished if we stopped trying to convince our fellowmen about the truth of our opinions based upon facts and sound logic. Naturally, I speak only of convincing arguments and not of intolerant dealing with the opinions of others, nor of the use of force or even of extinguishing thought.

I should like to report to you my discussion with Monsieur Miton about probability on the basis of notes I made that same evening. Of course I shall not render our talk verbatim; while writing down my own words, I have composed the sentences much more clearly than I would have been able to do during the discussion. For the sake of fairness I did the same with the words of M. Miton. Thus my drafts about our talk are not literal in the sense of court reportage, but I hope that our points of view are better mirrored in them than if I had repeated everything verbatim.

Our talk began with a conversation about our correspondence. First I told him briefly the contents of my three preceding letters. I defined probability as the degree of certainty, and emphasized that actually every probability is a conditional one, generally depending on the circumstances and changes in connection with them. I hinted that the relative frequency of an event fluctuates in a random manner around the fixed probability of this event. I emphasized further that his law holds only if the event in question is observed in a sequence of mutually independent experiments performed under the same conditions. As an example I mentioned the following case: An urn contains white and red balls in a given proportion. We repeatedly draw a ball from it and after each drawing replace the ball and shake the urn well in order to restore the original situation. Monsieur Miton's first remark referred to this example.

MITON:

I understand your excitement, Monsieur Pascal, in that you are the first to formulate this interesting fact. It seems to me, however, that this law can be applied only in a very restricted domain: apart from lottery and games of chance – in which I also am interested, although not so much as our mutual friend the Chevalier de Méré – I cannot imagine any other example where the conditions of your proposition would be fulfilled. You know, Monsieur Pascal, that I often go to the races,[18] not to win money – fortunately, I am not compelled to do that – but for the sake of company. But once there, I take a lively part in making bets and thus I know from my own experience that to know in advance which horse will win is just as impossible as to predict the result of dicing, depending as they both do on chance. In the case of horse races, however, your law cannot be applied; since even if a race were repeated with the self-same horses and riders (which in reality seldom occurs), it would not be the same race and the chances of the horses would not be exactly the same. Much depends on the condition of the horse and rider. Indeed, a horse may fall and break a foot or the rider may get hurt; even if the horse were able to race again, this does not happen without aftereffects.

PASCAL:

The validity of a law is not affected because its conditions are in certain circumstances not fulfilled, and thus the law cannot be applied at all. It becomes doubtful only if its conclusions happen to be false in a case where the conditions of its applicability are fulfilled. But you, Monsieur Miton, are, nevertheless, right in that random events do indeed exist where the occurrence or non-occurrence of them can be observed a single time only, since we can never observe them again. I call events of this kind *single random events*.

MITON:
Can the probability of a single random event thus not be determined empirically, i.e., by observing their relative frequency?

PASCAL:
In fact it is possible, since we can make a single observation only, and thus the value of the relative frequency is either 0 or 1.

MITON:
But what does the statement that its probability is equal to a certain number, say to 1/2, really mean for such a single random event?

PASCAL:
The sense of this statement is the same as in the case of events observed more than once. You know, for instance, the common practice when two children draw both ends of a forklike breast-bone until one of its ends breaks. During the pulling the children must wish for something; according to a naive belief, the child in whose hand the unbroken part remains can expect the fulfillment of his wish. Since the bone is symmetrical, the probability of winning is equal to 1/2 for both children, although of course one cannot repeat the play with the broken bone.

MITON:
In this example one can indeed say that your law holds, since if we observe this play many times, we shall see that the child holding the right or the left side of the bone, respectively, wins approximately in half of the cases. But in the case of horse racing there is no similar avoidance of the dilemma. In spite of this I also am of the opinion, even in the case of horse racing as well, that it is sensible to say that a given horse will win with a certain probability, let us say with the probability 1/2. As a matter of fact, spectators also seem to have a completely determined opinion about this question according to which they bet on the outcome of the running. The opinions of individuals, however, may largely differ according to their information with respect to the individual horses. Accordingly, it seems to me that, in general, different people allot different probabilities to the same event, and I do not see any principle by which I could decide which of them is right. When a certain horse reaches the goal first,

this proves not that those who bet on it have been right, but only that they were lucky. In connection with gambling all experts agree, but this is an ingenious exception. You, Monsieur Pascal, defined the probability of an event as its degree of certainty. It seems to me to be appropriate to modify this definition so that the probability of a random event should have a different, personal value for each person which shows how each judges the degree of certainty of the event in question. I believe that one cannot speak about the probability of an event any more than about the beauty of a poem, a picture, or a lady. *De gustibus non est disputandum*: One cannot dispute about matters of taste; tastes are simply different and, similarly, each judges the chances of a random event differently.

PASCAL:
I am of a different opinion. To my mind the probability of a random event has a well-determined value which does not depend on opinion, even if different individuals estimate this value differently. Naturally, when at the horse race somebody advises me to bet on a certain horse and then this particular horse wins, this fact in itself does not thereby mean that my adviser estimated the chances of the horses well. But if the tips of this adviser work well over a long time in most cases — say in some 90 percent — and the tips of another adviser are fulfilled only in some 10 percent of the cases — then I would assume that the tips of the first adviser should be followed and not those of the second.

MITON:
Naturally.

PASCAL:
Can we in this case then state that the personal opinions of the first advisers are more reliable than those of the second?

MITON:
Obviously.

PASCAL:
Now I have caught you! You acknowledge that the first adviser can judge the real probabilities at the horse race better than the second;

thus, there is reason to speak of the probability of the events in question with this example as well, although the exact values of these probabilities are now known to anybody and are differently estimated by different individuals according to their personal opinion.

MITON:

I acknowledge that your answer is a pretty one, although actually you are speaking of the probability of one event and I am speaking of the probability of another. You are speaking about the probability of the event that an expert gives a good tip and this is no longer a single event but an often repeatable one, and the value of this probability can approximately be determined by the observation of the relative frequency. But now let us leave the horse race, since it is not the example that is of importance for us but the general principle. Please explain to me how you can confirm that it really makes sense to speak about the probability of an event independently of the person who forms an opinion about it. I assume that every probability is subjective; if you, on the contrary, believe that there is reason to attribute an objective value to probability, then you must prove this to me.

PASCAL:

I am ready to allow that I cannot prove it. I consider it, namely, as an axiom and, as it is known, axioms cannot and need not be proved at all. I can only prove that these axioms are just as reasonable as other axioms whose validity is doubted by neither you nor by anyone else, and that the conclusions following from my axioms are consistent with our experience. You will perhaps be surprised if I indicate that the axiom of the objectivity of probability is nothing else than a natural and almost trivial extension of another axiom acknowledged by everybody.

MITON:
Which axiom are you thinking of?

PASCAL:
The axiom of causality, according to which all causes which influence a phenomenon together determine exactly the course of this phenom-

enon, and the same causes always have the same effects. This axiom cannot be proved either, just because of its fundamental character. Nevertheless, I suppose that you are not skeptical about the principle of causality, are you?

MITON:
Not really, although I have never been concerned about its being an unprovable axiom.

PASCAL:
It is unprovable, but it does not need any proof either; it is the basis of our scientific world concept, and every natural law disclosed by science is a new argument in favor of the validity and necessity of this axiom. But he who acknowledges the validity of the axiom of causality must also accept the other axiom according to which random events have a probability independent of us, i.e., an objective probability, since this is nothing else than a more precise formulation of the same fundamental principle.

MITON:
This is surprising indeed and not clear to me. Could you perhaps clarify it by an example?

PASCAL:
Most gladly. The generalization of the principle of causality can be formulated as follows: All the circumstances that may in their totality influence a phenomenon determine the course of this phenomenon unequivocally; when, however, only a fragment of these circumstances is known, then the course of the phenomenon is not, in general, unequivocally fixed, but there are many possibilities, each of them having a certain probability. By the randomness of an event we understand precisely the fact that the given circumstances do not unequivocally determine what will happen; certain events either may occur or may not occur, but the probabilities of both possibilities are determined. And this does not depend on whether or not we know the probabilities exactly or approximately or even at all, just as we do not always know the exact causal laws in connection with unequivocally determined phenomena. Since you wish an example, let us consider

44

the example of the pendulum which was studied by Galileo. If we know exactly the length and original position of the pendulum at the moment of its release, then we can calculate precisely (if we disregard the resistance of air and friction) the position of the pendulum at any given moment. But if we know, for instance, only the length and original position of the pendulum and do not know the exact time when it was released, then of course we cannot give exactly the position in which it will be at a given moment, but we can at least state that it will be on the left or on the right of its widest point, each with a probability equal to 1/2. More generally, we can calculate for each angle α the probability that at the moment of observation, the direction of the pendulum will deviate with an angle less than α from the perpendicular.

MITON:
I begin to understand your philosophy, but I am far from accepting it. If I understand you properly, you consider complete determination as a limiting case of the principle of the objectivity of probability.

PASCAL:
You understand it quite well. It is a limiting case and even one which in the real world can never be realized completely, but only approximately. As a matter of fact, we can never know exactly and can never consider all the circumstances that have an effect upon the phenomenon. In the above example I have said that we can describe exactly the movement of the pendulum if we disregard the resistance of air and friction. But these circumstances can never be completely excluded. Even if we put the pendulum under a glass bell which has had the air pumped out — as in the experiment which I performed following Torricelli — still there remains the friction, the vibration of the building in which we perform the experiment, and a whole series of other random circumstances. And the situation is similar to every law which we consider as exactly determined. As soon as the most important factors determining the phenomenon are known, the course of the phenomenon can be foreseen by and large, though certainly not in its every detail. Perhaps you remember my experiment for observing the weight of air. I succeeded in showing that upon a high summit — e.g., on the peak of the Puy de Dôme — the column of mercury is lower than at the foot of the mountain, the weight of the column of

air is smaller at the summit than down below. Still the pressure of air is far from being constant, even at a given place, since it depends on the weather, on the vapor content of air, etc., and all these factors are continuously changing in an unforeseeable manner. Thus, we cannot give exactly the pressure of air in Paris; we can only give certain limits between which the pressure will with great probability lie. These limits are determined by the geographical position of Paris and by the season; you can think about these what you like, but the column of mercury in the Torricelli experiment will not be raised or decreased by a hundredth part of an inch by your thoughts. We can take shooting stars for a further example. As is known, star showers are the most frequent in August. And this was the case even before it was observed by anybody. The number of shooting stars is not, therefore, greatest in August because we both are of this opinion, but the reverse: we are of the opinion because this happens to be so. Events occurring on the moon have also a well-determined probability, though none of us can have any personal opinion about it since we do not know at all what kind of events can happen there.

Miton:

You need not continue this enumeration since we are of the same opinion in these things. I agree with you that the probabilities of the inanimate world have an objective validity, indeed I never questioned this at all. But allow me the privilege of reminding you that you again directed the discussion to a terrain where you stand on firm ground: all your examples refer to experiments repeatable without limit, to events which can be often observed whenever you choose, where the value of the probabilities can be deduced from the determination of the relative frequency. My objections refer to single random events, such as the outcome of a horse race or shipwreck. I remain with my opinion that in such cases only subjective probability judgments are possible.

Pascal:

For the same reasons I am convinced that even single unique events have an objective probability and that they have a cause. Otherwise, I see — as to the objectivity of probability — no difference based on principle between events of lifeless and living Nature. In the degree that the principle of causality holds in living Nature, the probability of random events is objective as well, though the relations are here much more complex, and it is difficult to achieve a deep insight. Therefore, it is more difficult precisely to foresee events in living Nature. From this, however, it follows only that just in this domain the investigation of probabilities is of still greater importance. If you like, let us look at the problem of shipwreck somewhat more closely. Undoubtedly merchants and businessmen have their personal opinions about the probability that the ship will reach her place of destination intact. I have heard that in England the merchants often insure their wares transported on ships against their loss, that is, they pay a certain sum to a so-called insurance company, which then compensates the loss if a shipwreck or sea-robbery occurs; but if the cargo arrives at its destined port in good order, the company keeps the insurance fee paid in advance. In fixing the insurance fee, both the merchant and the insurance company clearly estimate the probability of the loss; both estimations are subjective. And in spite of this, I think it is quite reasonable to speak of the objective probability of the loss, even if nobody knows it exactly. It is not our opinion but this objective probability which has an influence upon the destiny of the ship. Suppose you believe a ship will sink and, in fact, she does; what would you then say if a law court called you to account for it? Would you not reject the accusation by saying that your opinion could not have had any influence at all upon the event? If I were the judge, I would immediately acquit you, but at the same time I would sentence you for your views about subjective probability. The profits of an insurance company eventually show how well it estimates the probabilitіеs of shipwrecks. If the company, however, does not judge correctly this real probability (which of course can change with time), it will soon become bankrupt either because it pays out more indemnities than it collects in insurance fees, or because it demands too high fees which the merchants do not want to pay.

MITON:
Monsieur Pascal, you are like a cat always falling upon its paws however it is thrown. You have managed again to change from single events to often observable events for which the relative frequency gives a reliable estimation of the unknown objective value of the probability.

PASCAL:

Be convinced, Monsieur Miton, that the reason is not my exceptional skill in discussion, which cannot be compared with your rhetorical art. My only advantage is the truth of my words.

MITON:

For your sake, I am ready to acknowledge that one can also ascribe to single random events an objective probability independent of our judgment though this value is unknowable. In my opinion, however, dealing with things which are essentially unattainable in our experience has nothing to do with science, and what we should understand by the "existence" of such things is above all a matter of question.

PASCAL:

Think of the existence of the atoms of Lucretius, which cannot be seen even under the microscope; still, by means of these atoms, we can explain everything in the world. We are dealing in both cases with scientific hypotheses which can be tested, not directly, but through the verification of the consequences deduced from them.

MITON:

Monsieur Pascal, you certainly are capable of holding your own as a lawyer; you apply most skillfully the method of the *argumentum ad hominem*. It seems to me that you have in mind our discussion in which I said that the *De rerum natura* is my favorite book, since I —like Lucretius—am an admirer of the goddess Venus. But you have not convinced me yet. Your comparison of probability and atoms is certainly worthy of reflection. You think, therefore, that the probability of a single event belongs to the things about which the poet says:

> Listen then further about bodies which are unavowedly part of the world and are yet not visible. Think first of the power of the wind. It lashes the water of the sea and sinks powerful ships and scatters the clouds .... Therefore what are the winds? They are indeed bodies not visible.[19] Do you think that blind winds and unknown probability together sink the unfortunate galleys?

PASCAL:

Yes, one could say this too, and Lucretius would certainly agree with this, since he was of the opinion that the world originated through random collisions of the atoms. Perhaps you remember the following lines:

> For certainly it was no design of the first beginnings that led them to place themselves each in its own order with keen intelligence, nor assuredly did they make any bargain as to what motions each should produce; but the multiplicity of atoms, because if many first beginnings of things, struck with blows and carried along by their own weight from infinite time unto this present, have been accustomed to move and to unite in all manner of ways, and to try all combinations whatsoever they could produce by coming together; thus it comes to pass, that being spread abroad through aeons, by attempting every sort of combination and motion, at length those come together which, being suddenly brought together, often become the beginnings of great things, like the earth, the sea, the sky, and living creatures.[20]

MITON:

I of course remember, and I remember also those passages where Lucretius compares the random movement of the primary elements with the dance of the grains of dust in the rays of the Sun.[21] Do you suppose that the calculus of probabilities could be used for the investigation of random phenomena like these?

PASCAL:

I am sure of it. I am convinced that the calculus of probabilities will make possible the mathematical investigation of natural phenomena which are not comprehended by other mathematical methods; I mean the random phenomena of Nature.

MITON:

You speak about chance as if one could always decide clearly whether an event is or is not random. It seems to me that the thing is not so unambiguous. What appears to be random to one must not appear to be random to another. Let us take your example of the pendulum. If you do not know when the pendulum has been started by me, the position of the pendulum in a given moment is random for you but not for me, since I know exactly when I have let it go. Accordingly, even about the randomness of an event there are only subjective judgments possible.

PASCAL:

I agree with you that one and the same event in certain cases can be considered as random, in others as causally determined; depending on the circumstances under which we investigate it, an event may be random, and if it is, then the same objective circumstances determine the probability of this event, too.

MITON:

Well, I shall not wrangle further with you about this problem; you have convinced me, anyhow, that your standpoint is consistent, well pondered, and undoubtedly these things can be treated from your point of view as well. But I still stick to my subjective probabilities since these I know, while I do not know what to make of your objective probabilities, even if I admit to their existence, since they are unknown to me. I have the feeling that you have described somebody to me in glowing terms whom I do not know, and now that, after being impressed by your enthusiasm, I wish to make his or her acquaintance, you are unable to introduce this person to me.

PASCAL:

Allow me to modify this metaphor somewhat. It seems to me, rather, that I have praised to you a writer of Greek antiquity whom I indeed cannot introduce to you but whose writings, which are not completely lost, are in large part bequeathed to us, and when you, after mastering the linguistic difficulties, study these works thoroughly, you will become acquainted with the writer as well, and you will be able to guess something about his lost writings. This of course would be no easy matter, but it would be worthwhile doing.

MITON:

I shall ponder these things. But tell me, Monsieur Pascal, do the theorems of the calculus of probabilities, for instance your theorems of addition and multiplication, hold only for objective probabilities or for subjective as well?

PASCAL:

Subjective probability judgments are often not numerical but are given only qualitatively. Even when a certain individual always formulates his subjective probabilities quantitatively, the rules mentioned are valid only if all the probability judgments of this person are in complete harmony and form a coherent consistent system. But I do not believe in the existence of such a man. Thus, even if you start from subjective probability judgments about events which form a certain starting point, it is reasonable to calculate — instead of judging — the probability of the composite event whose probability can be determined mathematically from the probabilities of the events serving for starting points. In this case, that is, you obtain a system of probabilities (if the beginning values are consistent) in which the general laws are completely valid; for, in this system, the probability of an event will have the same value as if the objective probability of each event of those forming the starting point would be equal to its subjective judged value. Thus, in this system the events mostly have empirically determinable probabilities; in this way, one can control and, if necessary, correct the subjective judgments chosen for the starting point.

MITON:
Thus, you still recognize — at least with respect to the starting points — the indispensableness of subjective probabilities?

PASCAL:
I see it differently. What you call subjective probability, I consider as a hypothesis.

MITON:
Is it not just a difference of words?

PASCAL:
And something more. I ascribe at the beginning no numerical values at all to these hypothetical probabilities, but denote them only by letters, say, x, y, z, and so forth, and try to determine the values of these magnitudes by observing the frequencies of other events having probabilities depending somehow on these magnitudes.

MITON:
It seems to me that eventually our opinions are not so very different after all, at least with respect to the practical consequences. Thus, I suggest that we not bore our friends further with our dispute; even if we continued it as long as we wished, a certain difference would

still remain between us, since we both are independent thinkers. Nevertheless, I believe that we agree in our views as nearly as possible, and thus all further dispute is superfluous. It seems to me that our fair ladies here are already annoyed with us for neglecting them; therefore, I suggest – if you have no objection – that we should conclude our conversation for this evening.

PASCAL:
As you please, Monsieur Miton.

Our discussion ran something like this. I add nothing to it, since everything I can say about your questions is contained in it. I beg you to let me know candidly your opinion about this discussion between Monsieur Miton and your most devoted admirer who esteems you more than anybody else,

Blaise Pascal

P. S. Lately I thumbed through the *Meditations* of Marcus Aurelius and by chance I happened to open the book at the passage where he writes that there are but two possibilities: either the world is ruled by a mighty chaos or by order and law. Should any of the two be realized, the thinking man has one thing to do: he must stand firm on the place designed for him by fate or by chance, like a rock in the sea on which the wild, foaming waves break. Although I have often read these lines before, I never realized till now how Marcus Aurelius takes it to be obvious that the world is ruled either by chance or by order and law, so that he believes that these two possibilities exclude each other. I am convinced that these two statements do not contradict each other; on the contrary, both of them are simultaneously true. The world is ruled by chance and, exactly for this reason, there exist order and law which emerge from an ocean of random events according to the rules of probability. This is the reason that I consider understanding the concept of probability a task of the highest importance, and I am for this reason engaged so passionately with these problems. However, I must not be too much concerned to explain this to you, since you were well aware, from the very first moment of our correspondence, that we are dealing here with something of far higher importance than mere gambling with dice.

LETTER TO THE READER

Dear Reader:

These lines are only to confess (appropriately in the form of a letter) something which you yourself have already found out without being told, namely, that Professor Henri Trouverien never lived and thus did not find out anything (as his very name indicates — Trouverien, which might be translated into English as Findsnaught). Therefore, of course, the Pascal letters, published above, were never written by Blaise Pascal. Perhaps you expect a kind of apology from me because I have chosen the form of fictitious Pascal letters in order to explain some principal problems of the probability theory. I do not think, however, that such an apology is necessary, since either you have read these letters with interest and, then, any explanation is superfluous, or you did not like the letters and your opinion cannot be changed by any explanation. Thus I have only to note that, in choosing a literary form, I was influenced by motives similar to those used in the writing of my *Dialogues* (see [10]); the only difference is that I have tried here another form. (Eventually, I combined the two forms since here and there I inserted brief dialogues into the letters.) The fictitious letter is a well-known literary genre. Its origin — like so many things — can be found in ancient Greece. In Plato's time the fictitious letter was a form often used for dealing with philosophical problems. This kind of fiction is still vital today. As an example let me mention Thornton Wilder's masterpiece, *The Ides of March* (1948). In choosing Pascal and Fermat as partners of this correspondence, I followed the same principle as in my *Dialogues*: I put the correspondence in the period when the concept of probability was born in order to present this concept to the reader *in statu nascendi*, in the very freshness of its becoming.

In these *Letters on Probability* as well as in my *Dialogues*, I have tried to preserve historical fidelity and to avoid every sort of anachronism as far as it has been possible. In order to emulate the style of those times as well as to increase the "authenticity" of the letters, I worked many of Pascal's thoughts and aphorisms into the text. Some passages coincide even literally (or with insignificant changes) with Pascal's words. The corresponding passages in Pascal's works are then given in the notes. In the *Letters* I often cited from the works of authors other than Pascal; all these citations are taken from works which were really known to Pascal; some of these (e.g., Montaigne's *Essays*) are known to have been his favorite reading.

Thus, dear reader, I have done everything that I could to make it credible that these letters could have been written by Pascal himself. Of course I did not want to throw dust in your eyes or to make you believe somehow that you have been reading the original letters of Pascal. Finally, concerning the thoughts occurring in the letters, I do not wish to pretend at all that Pascal really thought of them, though it is not impossible, and, at any rate, it is not refutable by historical arguments.

Perhaps you will ask why I did not "publish" Fermat's answers as well. This, of course, would have been possible; I thought it, however, superfluous since Fermat's answers — at least partially — can be reconstructed easily from Pascal's letters. Moreover, I find most convincing the arguments of Professor Trouverien as to how Fermat's answers were lost. With hearty thanks for your patience, I remain,

Yours sincerely,

Alfréd Rényi

APPENDIX

Blaise Pascal was born on June 19, 1623, in Clermont-Ferrand. His father, Étienne Pascal,was president of the court of finance in Clermont, a man of wide and thorough learning. His mother, Antoinette Bégon, died when Blaise was only three years old, so that he and his sisters were brought up by their father. His sister Gilberte, who was three years older, later married Étienne Périer; Jacqueline, who was two years younger than Blaise, retired after the father's death to the cloister of Port-Royal. Blaise did not attend school and did not study at a university either; he was taught exclusively by his father. As a young child, Pascal began to show he was endowed with an extraordinary talent and when he was sixteen he wrote his famous *Essai sur les coniques* [Essay on conic sections]. This work contains the famous theorem that the (three) points of intersection of opposite sides of a hexagon inscribed in a conic section lie in a straight line. In 1642, when he was nineteen years old, Pascal invented the calculating machine. In the following years he constructed seven models of this machine and a few of them have survived. At the exposition which was organized at Clermont-Ferrand in 1962 on the occasion of the Pascal tercentenary, one of these machines was on display. Another example is in the Mathematical and Physical Cabinet of the "Zwinger" [Tower] in Dresden. Pascal is rightly considered as one of the forerunners of cybernetics, since he recognized clearly the importance of the calculating machine that he invented. This is shown by his words: "The calculating machine displays effects which are closer to thinking than anything done by beasts."[22]

In 1646 Pascal made several versions of Torricelli's experiment and gave a complete explanation of the results; he showed that the pressure of air depends on the height above the level of the sea; he discovered the fundamental theorem of hydrostatics and the principle of the hydraulic press.

To understand why these experiments could evoke such a loud repercussion and such a passionate discussion, we must know that Torricelli's experiment refuted the Aristotelian doctrine of *horror vacui*, according to which a vacuum was impossible. Thus, these experiments dealt a grave blow to scholasticism. Pascal was completely aware that his and Torricelli's experiments were of revolutionary importance for scientific thinking, hence he performed them with exceptional care and thoroughness. He strongly criticized people who in respect to authority were blind against facts. The fragment of a preface to a planned but never realized treatise of Pascal on the vacuum ends as follows: "Thus without contradicting the ancients we can assert the opposite of what they say; and eventually whatever form this Antiquity may have said, the truth, when it is discovered in recent times, must always be preferred; it is always older than all opinions which people formed about it, and, therefore, it would be a grave misunderstanding about Nature to believe that She began to exist only when man began to discover her."[23]

In the problems of science Pascal stood firmly on the side of experimental method and unbiased logical thinking. But at the same time he was convinced that, in the domain of religion, thought does not suffice; in order to arrive at the truth, one needs here the help of faith.[24]

Religion played an enormous role in Pascal's world of ideas from the time of his "first conversion" in 1646. But for some years it was not the central theme of his life. Between the years 1652 to 1654, in his so-called profane period, he is described as a man of the world leading a dissolute life. In 1653 Pascal traveled to Poitou in the company of his good friends the Duke de Roannez, the Chevalier de Méré, and Monsieur Miton. It might have been during this journey that the Chevalier de Méré put his two questions about the games of chance over which Pascal and Fermat then exchanged letters in 1654. This correspondence was the birth of the probability theory.[25]

Pascal's first letter to Fermat was written on July 29, 1654, the second on August 24, 1654, the third, which consists of two lines only, on October 27, 1654. These letters, as it has already been said, deal with the two problems formulated by de Méré. The first runs as follows: How many times must one throw at least two dice so that the probability of throwing the *sonnez* (i.e., throwing two 6's at the same time) will be greater than 1/2? This problem was solved by the Chevalier himself. The second — not so easy — problem which he could not solve, runs as follows: Two players play a game of chance in which both have the same chances in each game; at the beginning each player stakes the same sum with the agreement that the winner of the first *n* games will obtain the whole stake. How should the sum be divided if they break off at any stage? Now suppose that the play is abandoned before the end; the first player has won *a* games and the second player *b* games.

One may get an impression about contents and style of these letters from the following introductory lines of Pascal's first (authentic) letter:

"Sir,

1. Like you, I am equally impatient, and although I am again ill in bed, I cannot help telling you that yesterday evening I received from M. de Carcavi your letter on the problem of points, which I admire more than I can possibly say. I do not have the leisure to write at length, but, in a word, you have solved the two problems of points, one with dice and the other with sets of games, with perfect justness; I am entirely satisfied with it for I do not doubt that I was in the wrong, seeing the admirable agreement in which I find myself with you now.

I admire your method for the problem of points even more than that for dice. I have seen several people obtain that for dice, like M. le Chevalier de Méré, who first posed these problems to me, as well as M. de Roberval: but M. de Méré never could find the true value for the problem of points nor a method for deriving it, so that I found myself the only one to know this ratio.

2. Your method is very sound and is the one which first came to mind in this research; but because the labor of the combination is excessive, I have found a shortcut and indeed another method which is much quicker and neater, which I would like to tell you about in a few words: for henceforth I would like to open my heart to you, if I may, as I am so overjoyed with our agreement. I see that truth is the same in Toulouse as in Paris."[26]

These letters only deal with the two questions of the Chevalier de Méré while the general problems of the calculus of probabilities are not mentioned; even the word "probability" does not occur at all.

From the same year, 1654, originate Pascal's works about the number triangle, named after him, and other related questions about combinations. His interest in combinations was aroused by his investigations in probability theory.

A little later, on November 23, 1654, came a decisive turning point in Pascal's life which is usually called his "second conversion".

The record, which he wrote on this night of religious ecstasy, he sewed up in his coat and always carried it with him as a keepsake.[27]

Before long Pascal threw himself with all of his energy into the theological fights about Jansenism and helped the Jansenists in their struggle against the Jesuits. He wrote nineteen letters, brilliant with wit, which have become famous as *Lettres Provinciales*, a masterpiece of French literature. Undoubtedly, this was Pascal's chief activity between 1654 and 1658. But Pascal did not definitely abandon mathematics, even after his second conversion. Between 1658 and 1659 he continued investigations about the cycloid which are of extraordinary importance, since by calculating the area and the center of gravity of a segment of the cycloid as well as through the calculation of the volume and center of gravity of the body originated by the rotation of the segment of the cycloid, he made a decisive step in the creation of the calculus. He did not extend his knowledge in these questions to applications beyond the calculation of the definite integrals connected with the cycloid; but his work contains *in nuce* the general method developed later by Leibniz. Leibniz himself emphasized that he arrived at the notion of the derivative because of Pascal's *Traité de sinus de quart de cercle*.

From the year 1658 comes Pascal's work *De l'esprit géométrique et de l'art de persuader*, which shows that he was also much ahead of his times in the recognition of the importance of the axiomatic method in mathematics. This can be seen from the following: "One must prove all statements, and to this end one can use only self-evident axioms and already proved or accepted propositions."[28] He furthermore advised that the definition itself should always be substituted instead of the defined word.

Pascal's best-known work is the collection of his thoughts which were published after his death and form the famous *Pensées*. From these thoughts let me cite but one which shows how vain it is in Pascal to separate the scientist from the moralist by trying to divide one from the other. "All our dignity consists of thinking . . . thus we must take care to think well; that is the moral principle."[29]

Here I cannot try, however, to draw a mere comprehensive picture of Pascal's interesting, contradictory personality or to analyze the psychological and historical course of his life so rich in changes, which are not always easy to understand from a distance of three hundred years; moreover, it is not the task of this book. Thus let me cite only some lines of the poet Endre Ady:

> I like all men am a star
> of mysterious light, strange and distant,
> a fleeing wisp of light,
> a fleeing wisp of light.*

Pascal's unfinished and contradictory lifework today shines as a faraway, mysterious star.

---

* Endre Ady, *Poems*. Introd. and trans. Anton N. Nyerges (Buffalo, N. Y. 1969), p. 201.

As I have already mentioned, Pascal's latest authentic letter to Fermat about the questions of the Chevalier de Méré was written October 27, 1654. Furthermore, I have hinted at the decisive turning point of his life on the night of November 23, 1654. Thus, if we assume that Pascal might have written some further letters to Fermat on probability, these ought to have occurred between October 27 and November 23, 1654. Namely, they could not have been written before October 27, since then we would find in the surviving letters some hints of the lost ones. But neither could they have been written after November 23, since after this day, Pascal's mind was certainly occupied with thoughts of an entirely different kind. Everything known to us from Pascal's biography excludes almost certainly that he returned after November 23, 1654, to the "mathematics of chance".

However, as to the weeks before November 23, 1654, it is quite reasonable to assume that in this period Pascal was indeed occupied by these questions. Thus for the dating of the lost letters we have a rather narrow range – approximately four weeks. Considering the time needed in those days for the delivery of letters, Pascal might scarcely have obtained the answer to his letter, written the latter part of October, before November 5. And even if he had written immediately, he could not have received the answer to this second letter before November 15. But one may assume – and this is a quite plausible assumption – that in this period Pascal was already so deeply engaged in the correspondence that, even before having the answer to his second letter in his hands, he had already written a third one as a sequel to the second, and that just after the reception of the answer to his second letter, that is, between November 15 and 20, he immediately dispatched a fourth one. The sending of further letters within the given dates is scarcely imaginable. (In order to shorten the distance, I contrived that Fermat sojourned in mid-November in Orléans, that is, closer to Paris. I should like to point out here that Pascal and Fermat never met.)

Thus the date of each letter – provided that Pascal wrote the four letters to Fermat within the four weeks mentioned – can be "calculated" to have been within one to two days.

We know that before November 23, 1654, Pascal lived in a very excited state of mind. This is mirrored in certain parts of the *Letters on Probability* (first of all, in the second part of the third letter, where Pascal relates his dream).

The theory of probability is a comparatively young branch of mathematics. Its development as an independent science began with the correspondence between Pascal and Fermat in 1654, but individual problems about games of chance had already been dealt with much earlier by some mathematicians. The Franciscan friar, Luca Paccioli (1445–1514), for instance, dealt with a problem on probabilities in his book *Summa de arithmetica, geometria, proportioni e proportionalità*, printed in Venice in 1494; but he arrived at a wrong solution. Somewhat later Geronimo Cardano (1501–1576) and Galileo Galilei (1564–1642) correctly solved some special problems of the probability theory. The notion of probability itself is still much older; it had played a role in Greek philosophy (cf., for example, the quotation from Plato in the second letter). The thought that Natural Laws prevail through an enormous number of random events emerged with the ancient Greek materialists; its most circumstantial treatment can be found in Lucretius' poem *De rerum natura*: the passages that are most important from our point of view are cited in the fourth letter, in the dialogue between Pascal and Miton (and in the notes). In modern times questions on gambling and especially on dicing had an important role in the development of the probability theory. In antiquity dicing was a very popular way to gamble and was, indeed, widespread. With respect to the history of the taxillus play in the second letter, I relied on the excellent work by Hagstroem [5]. The history of the probability theory from Pascal to Laplace was very thoroughly studied by J. Todhunter [13]; many interesting details are contained in the book of K. Jordan [14] and in the recent important monograph of F. N. David [28]. It is not our aim to present the history of the probability theory here, suggesting only the influence that the correspondence between Pascal and Fermat had upon the further development of this new branch of knowledge. In 1658 appeared the treatise by Christian Huyghens (1629–1695), *De Ratiociniis in Aleae Ludo* [Reasoning on games of chance] in which the questions studied by Pascal and Fermat are dealt with in detail, apparently upon the basis of the correspondence between Pascal and Fermat, although it deals with many similar problems also. The fundamental work *Ars conjectandi* [Art of conjecture = calculus of probabilities] [30], by Jacob

Bernoulli (1654–1705), which appeared posthumously in 1713, is closely connected to Huyghens's treatise. The first part of *Ars conjectandi* is an exposition of Huyghens's work with commentaries and additions and gives a complete treatment of all problems enumerated by Huyghens without solution. But the most important part of *Ars conjectandi* is the fourth, which deals with the law of large numbers. Pierre-Remond de Montmort's (1678–1719) *Essai d'Analyse sur les Jeux de Hasard* [Essay on the analysis of games of chance], written somewhat later but published (1708) earlier than Bernoulli's *Ars conjectandi*, is related to Huyghens and thus indirectly to the correspondence between Pascal and Fermat; the same can be said about Abraham de Moivre's (1667–1754) highly important work, *De Mensura Sortis, seu de Probabilitate Eventuum in Ludis a Casu Fortuito Pendentibus* [On the measure of chance or on the probability of the results in games of chance], which appeared in *Philosophical Transactions* in 1711.

Besides the problems of games of chance there were problems about mortality tables as well as insurance problems which were dealt with at the beginning of the probability theory. In London, the regular weekly registering of deaths began as early as 1592. John Graunt (1620–1674) was the first who in 1662 calculated, upon the basis of these records, the probability of mortality as a function of age. Some years later, Jan Hudde (1628–1704) and Jan de Witt (1625–1672) in Holland arrived at similar conclusions and applied these to the calculation of life annuities; these problems were more thoroughly studied later by Edmund Halley (1656–1742). Although it cannot be proved, it is reasonable to assume that Pascal was well aware of the obvious connection between the probability theory, on one hand, and mortality tables and insurance matters, on the other; accordingly, I allowed myself a brief hint at this connection (ship insurance) in the fourth of these *Letters*.

IV. On the Mathematical Concept of Probability

The origin of the mathematical notion of probability, as of every idea, was gradual and slow. In the letters of Pascal and Fermat, the notion of probability does not occur explicitly. Moreover, it is not probability which is chosen as a basic concept in the treatise of Huyghens but the expectation ("the value of the hope"). Huyghens defines the expectation in the following manner: "To have p chances of obtaining a, and q chances of obtaining b, chances being equal, is worth $\dfrac{pa + qb}{p + q}$" (cf. [30], p. 8, and [28], p. 116). The first definition of probability is found in Bernoulli's *Ars conjectandi*; according to Bernoulli, probability is "the degree of certainty, which is to the certainty as the part to the whole". Besides this definition of a more philosophical than mathematical character, Bernoulli's work contains the so-called classical definition of probability as well: "...The probability of an event is the proportion of the number of favorable cases to the number of all possible cases, where the individual cases are supposed to be equally possible." This definition of probability will not be found exactly in the cited form in *Ars conjectandi*; the above formulation belongs to Laplace (1749–1827). It is taken from his fundamental *Theorie analytique de la probabilité* [Analytical theory of probability], a work which summarizes the results of the classical probability theory and gives a decisive thrust to its further development. The same definition can be found in another work of Laplace (*Essai philosophique sur les probabilités* [Philosophical essay on probabilities] [31a], pp. 4, 7), which treats the principal problems connected with the notion of probability most clearly, thoroughly, and in a style which is delightful even to readers of our own day. Although the classical definition of probability given above does not explicitly occur in Pascal's authentic letters, I think that it is not too much of an anachronism to include it in the fictitious letters, since this definition was in fact implicitly applied by Pascal as well as by Fermat in the solution of de Méré's problems. This definition sufficed — at any rate, practically — as long as the probability theory was mainly concerned with problems of games of chance. But from a fundamental point of view, the definition is inadequate, though — as Pascal says in its justification in the second letter — it does not contain any *circulus vitiosus*.

As a matter of fact, the inconclusiveness of this definition is not that it contains a *circulus vitiosus*, a *petitio principii*, as it was—even in our day—often stated (cf., for example, [31], p. 178) but rather that, actually, it is no definition at all. Namely, it does not answer the question, What is probability? It gives merely a practical instruction in how to calculate probability in certain simple cases (or, with recent terminology, in "classical probability algebras").

The creators of the probability theory also considered it in this sense; they took Bernoulli's definition of probability according to which the probability of an event is equal to the grade of its certainty. Mostly, however, they did not think it at all necessary to define probability explicitly; they took probability for a basic idea, and, therefore, the meaning would not require any further explanation. With respect to the degree of mathematical development of that time, this is perfectly understandable, since in the eighteenth century, for instance, the notions of number, of function, or of limit value were also far from clear in the present sense; and, moreover, this was not felt as an insufficiency at all.

The fundamental change in the situation took place only in the nineteenth century, when the conceptual content of mathematics as well as the notion of mathematical rigor both went through a decisive transformation during the gradual development of our present view of mathematics and its relation to reality. According to the present view, every branch of mathematics must be developed axiomatically, as a closed and logically consistent abstract theory, the basic notions of which need not be defined and must not be provided with any other meaning than the one contained implicitly in the axioms.

A mathematical theory developed in this manner can be applied to the description of reality as an abstract model of certain aspects of reality. The consequent realization of the modern abstract view completely transformed mathematics itself and became the starting point of a rapid development. The theory of sets, the theory of real and complex functions, topology, abstract algebra, and functional analysis developed side by side: symbolic logic came into being; the whole of mathematics was in turmoil. Probability theory, however, was not touched by this enormous transformation and the consequent developments lingered for a remarkably long time—in fact, until the first decades of the twentieth century. Although in the nineteenth century Gauss, Laplace, Poisson, Chebyshev, Markoff,

Bertrand, Poincaré, and many other mathematicians arrived at a number of new results in probability theory, and, at the same time, the practical applications of probability theory in science and economics became highly significant, there was actually no essential progress in the direction of the foundations of the mathematical theory of probability.

Because of this lag most mathematicians at the beginning of the twentieth century did not consider probability theory as an organic part and, still less, as equal to mathematics, but rather as a problematical discipline between mathematics and physics or philosophy. In 1900 the problem of axiomatic foundations of the probability theory was taken up by David Hilbert in his famous enumeration of the most important unsolved problems of mathematics.

The first significant step toward the solution of this task was undertaken in 1919 by Richard von Mises (1883–1953) (see [15]). Although his suggestion proved later on to be unsuitable and today has only historical significance, the discussions originated by it have aroused the interest of many mathematicians. The task of the exact axiomatic establishing of probability theory was first solved in an appropriate manner by A. N. Kolmogorov (b. 1903) in 1933 (see [16]). As with every scientific discovery, Kolmogorov's theory had its forerunners, too (cf. [17]).

In Kolmogorov's axiomatic probability theory, the random events are represented by sets and the probability is a "normed measure" defined on these sets; the expectation in this theory is an (abstract) Lebesgue integral. By developing probability theory upon a set theoretical, or more precisely upon a measure-theoretical basis, Kolmogorov has not only given a logically consistent foundation for the probability theory, but at the same time, he has joined it to the mainstream of modern mathematics and made possible the application of the highly developed modern branches of mathematics in probability theory. Kolmogorov's theory has been accepted because of its simplicity and advantages generally, and in the last thirty years has become the firm basis of research in probability theory.

Certain theoretical problems in physics concerning probability (e.g., quantum mechanics), of statistics, etc., made necessary the generalization of Kolmogorov's theory and the introduction of conditional probability spaces (see [18]); this logical development of his theory was already pointed out by Kolmogorov, but he did not follow these ideas further.

The explanation of the foundations made possible a rapid progress in the pure mathematical aspects as well as in the application of the probability theory. Since then probability theory has literally developed tempestuously, and its domain of application is ever widening.

V. A Further Letter to the Reader

Dear Reader,

When I reread my first letter to you, I realized that it needed an ending. That is, I explained in it only why I had chosen the form of fictitious letters for my story, but I did not tell you how I came upon the idea of dealing with these problems at all. I shall now remedy this omission with this second letter.

In part IV of the appendix I mentioned that today mathematicians essentially agree about the problems of the mathematical theory of probability. With respect to some problems of principle, however, the same cannot be said at all. These problems refer to the relation of the concept of probability to reality as well as to the applicability and interpretation of the theorems of the probability theory. Hence these are not pure mathematical questions; essentially, these are problems of a philosophical, epistemological nature and, thus, it is not surprising that they are still disputed today. Nobody who wishes to learn the probability theory thoroughly or who wishes to apply it successfully in some practical domain can disregard these problems, even less anyone who wants to understand clearly the uses of the probability theory and the possibilities it offers to scientists and practitioners.

My experiences in teaching probability theory on different levels to students of different interests and qualifications, as well as the experiences which I had while engaging in application of the probability theory to different domains, have taught me that it is not enough (though, of course, it is necessary) to have a suitably deep understanding and study of the mathematical theory to be able to immerse oneself thoroughly into the mathematics of the probability theory and apply it successfully; beyond that, it is absolutely necessary to have an appropriate mastery of the characteristic way of thinking about the probability theory.

In order to achieve this, one must first get more closely acquainted with some concrete possibilities of the application of the probability theory, and then strive to acquire a clear and thoroughgoing understanding of the fundamental problems connected with the concept of probability. This little volume is intended as an aid to achieving this latter aim.

The elements of the probability theory which are necessary to the understanding of the fundamental problems mentioned can be found in these letters on probability. I hope that for you, dear Reader, they were understandable even if you never before had anything to do with probability theory; in this case, I would be glad if reading this booklet would inspire you to a deeper acquaintance with probability theory. Although the problems dealt with here are understandable without any special mathematical knowledge, this does not mean that they are easy; their difficulty, however, is rather of a logical than of a mathematical nature; that is, these problems can be dealt with even on the basis of very simple exercises in probability. Therefore, one cannot simply reject the hypothesis that Pascal and Fermat once pondered over these problems and tried to give an answer to them. In this sense, therefore, it is far from being an anachronism that in this booklet Pascal expresses his views about all these problems.

The problems in question — as it has already been mentioned — are of an epistemological nature and are closely connected with the fundamental problems of scientific knowledge. Naturally, dear Reader, I am far from pretending that I have given a final solution to these problems disputed for hundreds of years. My aim was much more modest: I simply wished to present them in a clearly understandable manner. Of course, I have sometimes not avoided expressing my own views, chiefly in the fourth letter.

The views represented by Monsieur Miton were first formulated by de Morgan in 1847; according to this interpretation, every statement about the probability of an event is necessarily subjective; hence it depends on the individual who expresses the statement, and it represents the degree of accuracy of the individual's guess about the occurrence of this event. Thus probability is a measure of the individual's conviction. Although nowadays most mathematicians studying probability theory attribute an objective meaning to probability, there are some renowned modern mathematicians who still represent the subjective view (cf., for example, [19], [20], [21]). I think it is not necessary to emphasize — you may have discovered this already — that in this question I agree with Pascal's views.

If you want to learn more about these questions and if you want to study the different views about the concept of probability more thoroughly, I suggest you first read, in addition to those already listed, the works in the bibliography under numbers [22] to [27].

Finally, I should like to emphasize that the fundamental problems of probability theory are closely connected with certain basic problems of mathematical statistics and information theory. (Thus, for instance, in the dispute about the question of objectivity or subjectivity the so-called Bayesian method plays a central role.) Within the given framework of this booklet it was not possible to discuss problems like these. Perhaps I shall again have the opportunity to write about these problems, too. Till then, I send you my good wishes.

Yours,

Alfréd Rényi

Unfortunately, we shall never read the continuation, promised in the last letter of the present booklet, of Rényi's delightful and witty writings about the problems of probability. On February 1, 1970, the author died after a brief illness at the age of only 49 years.

Alfréd Rényi was born on March 20, 1921, in Budapest. His father was an engineer, a man of wide learning; his mother was the daughter of Bernát Alexander, professor of philosophy and aesthetics at the University of Budapest and a most influential philosophical writer at the turn of the century and in the following years. Later in his life, Rényi liked to hint that his grandfather was an inspirer of his philosophical and literary tastes; and actually, the free and elegant spirit of his essays and dialogues has much in common with the style of his famous forebear.

In his youth Rényi attended a humanistic middle school and throughout his life maintained an active interest in ancient Greek culture. In 1939 he was enrolled in the University of Budapest, but, being brutally dragged to a so-called labor camp in 1944, was prevented from finishing his studies. Fortunately, he succeeded in escaping and hiding with false papers for about half a year. After the Liberation (1945), he continued his studies at the University of Szeged and took his Ph. D. degree in 1945 under F. Riesz, one of the foremost masters of mathematics in our time.

In 1946–47 Rényi studied as a postgraduate student in the Universities of Moscow and Leningrad; at the latter he worked with Yu. V. Linnik toward the solution of Goldbach's hypothesis. By developing an idea of Linnik's, he discovered a method which, in the words of one of the greatest authorities in this field, Pál Turán, "can at present be regarded as one of the strongest methods of analytical number theory".*

In 1949 Rényi was appointed professor at the University of Debrecen; in the same year he became a corresponding member and in 1956 a regular member of the Hungarian Academy of Sciences. In 1952 he organized the chair of probability theory at the University

* Pál Turán, "Alfréd Rényi" (obituary). *Magyar Tudomány* 15: 579—80 (1970).

of Budapest. At the same time he was director of the Mathematical Institute of the Academy, a post he had held since its foundation in 1950. Under his wise and dynamic leadership the Institute became the heart of mathematical research in Hungary, and in the sixties it developed into something like an international mathematical center; he organized postgraduate courses for students of the developing countries, received mathematicians from all over the world, and edited a periodical well known and highly esteemed everywhere in mathematical circles.

Twice, in 1949 and in 1954, Rényi won the Kossuth Prize, the highest Hungarian prize given for outstanding intellectual achievement. More than 350 publications, among them several textbooks, attest his stupendous and versatile scientific activity. "Many of us", wrote Konrad Jacobs, "know him as one of the important number theorists of our time, a collaborator of P. Erdős and P. Turán. But Rényi also made important contributions to combinatorial analysis and graph theory, integral geometry and Fourier theory. Above all, he found his way into probability theory at a very early stage, his first paper dating from 1948. His contributions to probability theory are deep, original, and multiversal: mixing sequences, conditional probability spaces, and information theory are only a small selection of Rényi's themes."* In fact, Rényi had a rare sense both for pure and for applied mathematics. He developed an axiomatic theory of conditional probability spaces which is a natural generalization of A. N. Kolmogorov's axiomatic theory of probability, and at the same time he achieved important practical results in the theory of stochastic processes.

The relations of pure and applied mathematics interested him also from a general point of view; he discussed the problem in several essays and in some witty dialogues. Similarly, he used to emphasize the historical and philosophical aspects of mathematics in research as well as in teaching, and by his brilliant popular writings he contributed much to the spreading of mathematical culture in this country.

His open mind and charming personality gathered not only pupils and a whole school around him but also won him many friends all over the world. His frequent visits and travels abroad as well as his

---

* Konrad Jacobs, "Alfréd Rényi." *Zeitschrift für Wahrscheinlichkeitstheorie*, no. 4, 16 (1970).

longer sojourns brought him into contact with leading mathematicians of our day, some of them of Hungarian birth. He studied in the Soviet Union; at the beginning of the sixties he lectured on probability theory in France; in 1963–64 he accepted an invitation to the University of Michigan and also lectured in Canada; in 1968–69 he was visiting professor at Cambridge University. If we add to this breadth of experience his exceptional knowledge of languages as well as his thorough familiarity with research in his field, we understand that, as David Kendall says, "he made the integral and connected character of European mathematics—Europe in the widest sense, east and west—once more a reality".*

* David Kendall, "Alfréd Rényi" (obituary). *Journal of Applied Probability* 7: 509–522 (1970).

NOTES

(Numbers in brackets refer to Bibliography)

1. An allusion to Pascal's letter to Fermat, October 27, 1654, see [1], p. 90.
2. Cf. Pascal's letter to Fermat, August 10, 1660, see [1], pp. 522–23.
3. "Celeberrimae Matheseos Academiae Parisiensi", see [1], pp. 73–74.
4. The Latin original reads as follows: "et sic matheseos demonstrationes cum aleae incertitudine jungendo, et quae contraria videntur conciliando ab utraque nominationem suam accipiens stupendum hunc titulum jure sibi arrogat: aleae Geometria."
5. See [1], p. 1156.
6. See [1], pp. 1105–07.
7. See [1], p. 1147.
8. See Pascal's letter to Fermat, July 29, 1654; cf. [1], p. 77.
9. See Pascal's letter to Fermat, July 29, 1654; cf. [1], p. 77; cf. further note 26.
10. See [1], p. 710.
11. See [8], Rule III, p. 306.
12. See [4], p. 185. "... I am of opinion that what is not to be done by reason, prudence, and address, is never to be affected by force."
13. See [9], V., 38, pp. 220–21; or [9a], p. 224.
14. See [8], p. 318. In Rule IV Descartes characterizes mathematics as follows: "... I discovered finally that one must include in mathematics everything in which one investigates order or measure, and that it does not matter much whether the measure looked for refers to numbers, figures, stars, sounds or to any other object; so that one must obtain a general science which explains everything concerning order and measure, without concrete applications to any particular matter."
15. See [4], p. 146. "I leave the choice of my arguments to fortune, and take that she first presents to me; they are all alike to me, I never design to go through any of them; for I never see all of anything: neither do they who so largely promise to show it others."
16. See [7], (29 B, C), p. 53.
17. See [6], book IV, verses 961–64, pp. 316–17.
18. I have consciously used here a certain anachronism: Horse racing was introduced into France only after the death of Pascal; in England, however, it was popular at a much earlier date.
19. See [6], book I, verses 269–72, 277, pp. 20–21, 22–23.
20. See [6], book V, verses 419–31, pp. 368–71.
   Pascal could have cited here the following verse of Lucretius from Loeb Classical Library; see [6], book V, verses 187–94, p. 353:

"For so many first-beginnings of things in so many ways, smitten with blows and carried by their own weight from infinite time unto this present, have been wont to move and meet together in all manner of ways, and to try all combinations, whatsoever they could produce by coming together, that it is no wonder if they fell into such arrangements withal, and came into such movements, as this sum of things now shows in its course of perpetual renovation."

He could have also cited verses 1021–30 from book I ([6], p. 75), which agree almost word for word with those cited in the text: "For certainly neither did the first-beginnings place themselves by design each in its own order with keen intelligence, nor assuredly did they make agreement what motions each should produce; but because being many and shifted in many ways, they are harried and set in motion with blows throughout the universe from infinity, thus by trying every kind of motion and combination, at length they fall into such arrangements as this sum of things consists of; and this being also preserved through many great cycles of years, when once it has been cast together into convenient motions . . ."

21. Miton hints here at the following verses of Lucretius ([6], book II, verses 114–24, p. 93):

"Do but apply your scrutinizing when the sun's light and his rays penetrate and spread through a dark room: you will see many minute specks mingling in many ways throughout the void in the light of the rays, and as it were in everlasting conflict troops struggling, fighting, battling without any pause, driven about with frequent meetings and partings; so that you may conjecture from this what it is for the first-beginnings of things to be ever tossed about in the great void. So far as it goes, a small thing may give an analogy of great things, and show the tracks of knowledge." I certainly do not know any more poetical description of the Brownian movement of microscopic particles.

22. See [1], p. 1146.

23. See [1], p. 535.

24. See [1], p. 1222.

25. The correspondence between Pascal and Fermat was published in Fermat's *Complete Works* (see [29]), and, in English translation, in an appendix to the interesting book of Florence David [28] on the history of probability theory. Pascal's first letter to Fermat is lost; Fermat's (undated) answer has survived. We also have Pascal's second letter dated July 29, 1654; Fermat's answer (addressed to Carcavi) to this, dated August 9, 1654; Pascal's third letter, August 24, 1654; Fermat's letter, August 29, 1654, which crossed the former; and his answer to Pascal's third letter, September 25; finally, Pascal's fourth (original) letter, October 27, 1654. According to David, the solution of de Méré's problems (and herewith the theoretical foundation of the calculus of probabilities) is due to Fermat; her reasoning, however, is not completely convincing. The witty solution of the problem of rightful distribution comes certainly from Pascal, and this, a recursive procedure making superfluous the actual counting of the individual cases, is in itself a significant contribution to the foundation of probability theory.

26. See [1], p. 77; [28], pp. 230–31. For the last sentence, cf. also [30], p. 137.
27. The text of this famous Mémorial can be found in [1], pp. 553–54.
28. See [1], p. 597.
29. See [1], pp. 1156–57.

BIBLIOGRAPHY

[1] Pascal, Blaise, *Oeuvres complètes*. Text annotated by Jacques Chevalier. Bibliothêque de la Pléiade. Paris: Gallimard, 1954.

[2] Mesnard, J., *Pascal*. Paris: Hatier, 1951.

[3] Béguin, A., *Blaise Pascal in Selbstzeugnissen und Bilddokumenten*. Hamburg: Rowohlt, 1959.

[4] Montaigne, Michel Eyquem de, *Essays*. Translated by Charles Cotton. Edited by W. Carew Hazlitt. Chicago, London, Toronto: Encyclopaedia Britannica, Inc., 1952.

[4a] Montaigne, Michel de, *Les essais* (vols. 1–6). Texte du manuscript de Bordeaux. Étude, commentaires et notes par A. Armaingaud. (Text of Bordeaux Manuscript. Study, Commentaries and Notes by A. Armaingaud.) Paris: Conard 1924–27.

[5] Hagstroem, K. G., *Les préludes antiques de la théorie des probabilités*. Stockholm: C. E. Fritzes K. Hovbokhandel, 1942.

[6] Lucretius, *De rerum natura*. With an English translation by W. H. D. Rouse. London: D. Heinemann, 1966 (first printed 1924).

[7] Plato, *Timaeus. Critias. Cleitophon. Menexenus. Epistles*. With an English translation by R. G. Bury. (Loeb Classical Library, Plato, *Works*, vol. 7.) London: Heinemann, 1961.

[8] Descartes, René, "Règles pour la direction de l'esprit", in *Oeuvres choisies de Descartes*. Paris: Garnier, pp. 293–383.

[8a] Descartes, René, *Oeuvres*. Published by Charles Adam et Paul Tannery. Vol. 10. Physico-mathematica. — Compendium musicae. — Regulae ad directionem ingenii. — Recherche de la verité. — Supplément à la correspondence. New ed. Paris: Vrin, 1966.

[8b] Beck, L. J., *The Method of Descartes. A Study of the Regulae*. London: Oxford University Press, 1952.

[9] Cicero, M. T., *Gespräche in Tusculum*. Introduction and translation by Karl Büchner. Zürich: Artemis-Verlag, 1952.

[9a] Cicero, M. T., *Ciceronis Tusculanarum Disputationum*. Leipzig: B. G. Teubner, 1873.

[10] Rényi, Alfréd, *Dialogues on Mathematics*. San Francisco, Cambridge, London, Amsterdam: Holden-Day, 1965.

[11] Wilder, Thornton, *Ides of March*. 1948.

[12] Rényi, Alfréd, "Blaise Pascal, 1623–62." *Magyar Tudomány* 8: 102–108 (1964) (in Hungarian).

[13] Todhunter, J., *A History of the Mathematical Theory of Probability from the Time of Pascal to That of Laplace*. Cambridge and London: MacMillan, 1865. Reprint. New York: Chelsea Publishing Company, 1949.

[14] Jordan, K., *Fejezetek a klasszikus valószínűségszámításból* [Chapters from the classical calculus of probabilities]. Budapest: Akadémiai Kiadó, 1956 (in Hungarian).

[15] Von Mises, R., *Wahrscheinlichkeit, Statistik und Wahrheit.* 2nd ed. Vienna: Springer, 1936.

[16] Kolmogorov, A. N., *Foundations of the Theory of Probability.* New York: Chelsea, 1956. *Grundbegriffe der Wahrscheinlichkeitsrechnung.* Berlin: Springer, 1933.

[17] Rényi, Alfréd, *Probability Theory.* Budapest: Akadémiai Kiadó, 1970.

[18] Rényi, Alfréd, "On a New Axiomatic Theory of Probability", *Acta Math. Acad. Sci. Hung.* 6 : 285–335 (1955).

[19] De Finetti, B., "La Prévision: ses lois logiques, ses sources subjectives", *Ann. Inst. Henri Poincaré* 7 (1937).

[20] Savage, J. L., *The Foundations of Statistics.* New York: Wiley, 1954.

[21] *Studies in Subjective Probability.* Edited by H. E. Kyburg and H. E. Smokler. New York: Wiley, 1964.

[22] Carnap, R., *Logical Foundations of Probability.* Chicago: University of Chicago Press, 1950.

[23] Borel, É., *Probabilité et certitude.* Paris: Presses Universitaires de France, 1956.

[24] Good, I. J., *Probability and the Weighing of Evidence.* London: Griffin, 1950.

[25] Kolmogoroff, A. N., *Mathematische Wahrscheinlichkeit.* Grosse Sowjetenzyklopädie, 14, Leipzig: B. G. Teubner Verlagsgesellschaft, 1955, pp. 3–7.

[26] *Théorie des probabilités. Exposé sur ses fondements et ses applications.* Paris: Gauthier-Villars, 1952.

[27] Pólya, G., *Mathematics* and *Pllausible Reasoning.* Vol. 2. *Patterns of Plausible Inference.* Princeton: Princeton University Press, 1954.

[28] David, Florence N., *Games, Gods and Gambling.* (The origins and history of probability and statistical ideas from the earliest times to the Newtonian era.) London: Griffin, 1962.

[29] Fermat, P. de, *Oeuvres.* Vol. 2. Published by P. Tannery et C. Henry. Paris: Gauthier-Villars, 1894.

[30] Bernoulli, Jakob, *Wahrscheinlichkeitsrechnung* [Ars conjectandi]. Ostwald's Klassiker der exakten Wissenschaften, no. 107. Leipzig: Wilh. Engelmann, 1899.

[31] Laplace, P. S. de, *Philosophischer Versuch über die Wahrscheinlichkeit.* Ostwald's Klassiker der exakten Wissenschaften, no. 233. Leipzig: Akademische Verlagsgesellschaft m. b. H., 1932.

[31a] Laplace, P. S. de, *Essai philosophique sur les probabilités,* I–II. Paris: Gauthier-Villars, 1921.